SYRUP, BISCUITS AND SOW BELLY

Samuel B Mills

2015

ISBN: 1508944997
ISBN 13: 9781508944997

Dedicated to:

Mama Loziane Trawick Mills

My Wife Connie Harman Mills

The Two Who Touched and Shaped My Life the Most

ACKNOWLEDGEMENT

Thanks to Gloria Roberts Cannon Franklin who spent many hours proofreading this narrative. This long-time friend with her patient, plodding manner got the job done, and we had many laughs doing it.

CONTENTS

PROLOGUE

U.S. citizens born in the mid-1930s, '40s and '50s were blessed with unbelievable timing and grew up in possibly the best period our country has known financially, morally and culturally, traits which ensured a solid foundation for coming of age. Coming out of WW II, Seminole County and the country could better produce more marketable products compared to other nations. With a major portion of the world's production capability destroyed, countries purchased the United States' food and goods. In virtually every industry, businesses thrived and society prospered with local veterans starting out owning little and becoming prosperous farmers through grueling work and capable management.

Accordingly, cheap energy from the production of oil in abundance resulted in gas at under twenty cents per gallon, a price which made cars more affordable and supported the development of the United States interstate highway system.

Returning home to marry and raise families, veterans precipitated a housing construction boom. During the '50s, "mortgage hill," the brain child of Rupert Sheffield, provided housing for the middle class in Donalsonville, Georgia.

Experiencing full employment levels at a fair wage, citizens of Seminole County, Georgia, largely eliminated any need for welfare. Taking care of the indigent and providing reasonably priced health care, doctors had roles of leadership. When they identified legitimate needs, churches and families stepped in to furnish additional assistance.

Divorcing a spouse was a last alternative: most couples were devoted to their families for the sake of the children and searched for ways to give and take. Often friends and neighbors would treat spouses who divorced like outcasts through disassociation and speaking of the divorcees in harsh terms.

Children learned the right values at homes, schools and at churches, emphasizing love of country, family, neighbors and God. When loved ones passed away, friends and neighbors came together to hold wakes to support the grieving families. If a person needed to borrow an item, or required assistance with a task which exceeded a family's capabilities, friends came to the fore. The love in the neighborhoods, supported by the low crime level, created trust as shown by unlocked houses and cars. With a minimum of substance abuse, the justice system processed a relatively small number of alcohol and drug-related crimes.

A senior class trip to Washington in the '50s, which resulted in a class member becoming drunk in transit, marked the end of those excursions. Astonished that the calamity could happen, the school board and the community dealt firmly with the embarrassment.

If Johnny misbehaved and received a paddling at school, parents supported the punishment because the teachers had respect at school and in the county. Rule breakers often received another "correction" at home if the news of the incident made it to the parents. Children followed the rules or teachers administered consequences, often including spankings in a no tolerance manner. By focusing on educating the kids and avoiding kicking them to the next grade, children made better grades. If they failed to cut the mustard, the instructors stopped their advancement at the eighth grade, thereby putting pressure on mamas and daddies to counsel kids and become involved with their education.

In the rare case of unexpected pregnancies, the family and the young ones involved felt shame. The young woman would "go see an aunt" for a while and return, with or without the child, the disposition dependent on the consideration of adoption. The disgrace helped control the number of teenage pregnancies and resulted in instances of anxious parents ordering the expectant couple to marry under the "threat of a shotgun."

Annual family reunions, when extended families came together, visited and ate home cooking, communicated the importance of bloodlines. The fellowship, the renewal of friendships and the refreshing of roots provided the glue that cemented relationships.

Utilizing work as a character builder, parents taught children the importance of responsibility and self-reliance. With minimum labor-saving machines and tools available, people did the bulk of work by hand causing the expression, "Work is its own reward," to be commonly heard within families.

Arguing with a parent seldom occurred, as mamas and daddies expected children to show reverence to them and others. Kids witnessed their parents working diligently and cooperated out of admiration for the parents keeping the family on sound financial footing, so when mama or daddy said, "Do it," young folks complied with no back talk. If a "smart" comment erroneously erupted, the child could see "stars" from a slap across the face.

Residents had the joy of seeing innovations arrive, which the community had never known, such as the Tastee Freeze which drew the teenagers with its attractive glass front, abundant parking space, drinks and food. Sitting in the parking area, having a Coke, shooting the breeze with friends and listening to the juke box blaring out the current hits was a common way to spend a Friday or Saturday night.

Residents largely escaped the "ugliness of life" prevalent in the life of the 21st century: drugs, binge drinking, orange jumpsuits along the roadways, divorced and absent parents. In their futures the people of the era would better understand the toll those negatives could take on their lives and the lives of friends and family.

The following collection of stories depicts my view of growing up in and moving beyond this era with life's cornucopia of thistles and cupcakes:

CHAPTER 1

THE FAMILY

In the early morning hours of October 24, 1945, Dr. Harry Bryan Baxley delivered Samuel Baxley Mills. Doing the naming, Mama chose Samuel from Daddy and Baxley from the delivery man. Mama, along with numerous others in the county, loved and respected Dr. Baxley who had served in WWII and witnessed terrible horrors while recognizing his toughness. With a pleasant demeanor, a stranger would never suspect the doctor's exposure to the wounds of battles and the associated emotions.

Arduous work, positive living and the nourishment of my mental capabilities in school hallmarked my trip through "Eden." Starting out in a spot behind the eight ball as others, I made the best of whatever God-given potential and talents He bestowed on me. Not being described by my classmates as popular or Mr. Personality, they would probably admit that I was a serious-minded straight shooter who maintained an untarnished nose, so to speak.

The place I called home was in South Georgia near a town with a population of about two hundred called Iron City which was located four miles from Donalsonville, the county seat of Seminole County.

Parents saw this agricultural community as a decent setting in which to raise a family and prepare the children for those next steps in life. The residents, possessing integrity and moral fiber learned in the churches and from families, tried to do and support the right things to generate happiness and prosperity.

The Rock Pond voting district, named for Rock Pond, a small lake with a generous quantity of moccasins, rattlesnakes, live oaks and cypresses, is where the Mills family resided. Over the years the fertilizer run-off from adjacent farm lands caused pollution which killed the aquatic life, thereby destroying a productive fishing hole.

The Rock Pond Primitive Baptist church, established in 1842, where Mama, Daddy and two brothers lie at rest, resides adjacent to the pond. Through Mama's membership, the church has reserved plots for Connie and me when our journey is finished. Mama, grandparents, great-grandparents and probably great-great-grandparents joined the church and have adjoining gravesites in the cemetery, or close by.

My great-great-grandfather Othneil Trawick lived in the mid-1800s on the land north of the church. Great-grandfather George inherited a portion of the land after Othneil's death, but George passed at the age of 26, leaving a widow and two male children. Ironically, great-great-grandfather Othneil's widow lived down the road so both women had to buck up and deal with the loss of the man of the house. Great-grandfather George left two sons Emory and Will to carry on the name and farm the land.

In a rare occurrence for the period, widowed great-grandmother Trawick had an unplanned child named Harvey. The loneliness of the farm, hardships and the presence of a doctor who provided "other services" during house calls set the stage for an illegitimate birth. Harvey, born in an unfavorable light, was given the last name of Trawick but was not as solidly a part of the family as if legitimacy had prevailed.

After he left home, Harvey relocated to Havana, Florida, where he became a strong player in the lumber business. Harvey's brother Emory joined him for a while, but he subsequently returned to the farm. During Granddaddy Emory Trawick's Florida time, Grandmother Chloe gave birth to Mama near Hinson, Florida, a town adjacent to Havana.

In the '50s and '60s, Mama traveled to Tallahassee, Florida, to see Aunt Lillian, Harvey's widow, whom she liked visiting to maintain the connection to the bygone days. Because Harvey had the stigma of illegitimacy, other family relations had disassociated from the woman. Leaving Aunt Lillian comfortable in a charming brick home proved that Harvey's long term business life had produced wealth in spite of a murky heritage.

Will and Emory both married Spooners from the same family of great-granddaddy Joseph Spooner. Joseph had ten children with his first wife, including Grandmother Chloe Spooner Trawick; then he had a last child by his second wife Margaret Gainey after his first wife died. The huge family was because of children being a primary source of labor in the agrarian society.

Having a distinctive heritage, the Spooner name tracks back to the Mayflower via the Warren's family. Richard Warren was one of twenty-three pilgrims who came on the Mayflower and settled in what is now Massachusetts. He and his wife Elizabeth Marsh bore a son Nathaniel who married Sarah Walker and produced a daughter Sarah Warren who married John Blackwell in 1674. Their daughter Desire Blackwell was the wife of Lettis Jenny of Dartmouth, Massachusetts. The Jennys had a daughter Sarah Jenney who married Simpson Spooner in 1724. The Spooner name and heritage perpetuated from there. What is most interesting is that their daughter Deborah Spooner married a cousin Joseph Spooner in 1748. With a shortage of men, it was common for relatives to marry in the era.

With only blood-related neighbors within a mile of our residence, including four great uncles and aunts on the Spooner side and great-aunt Lila Mae Spooner Youmans, the fruit of Joseph Spooner's second marriage, a pleasant sense of belonging prevailed. Mama's brother and family plus five double first cousins and families on the Trawick side resided nearby, and a sister and family lived three miles away in Iron City.

3

The Spooners and Trawicks enjoyed a reunion each July that was attended by the spawn of the two families. The Spooner-Trawick marriages had yielded seventeen double first cousins, so these get-togethers brought in numerous kin, with many traveling a significant distance. Looking forward to the affair every year, relatives shared delicious food with fellowship and regenerated the love that bound them.

Settling in the county in the mid-1800s, both families produced numerous relatives over the years to an extent that maintaining wide family contacts became difficult. The joke was that the families were related to the all of the whites in the county and some from other races. With such a preponderance of relatives and the closeness of bloodlines, holding family secrets closely proved unwieldy. The "closet door" seemed to stand open always, exposing the "skeletons" and their locations.

Joe Spooner lived large in the tough times of the late 19th and the first part of the 20th century, and in the vernacular of the day, the title of plantation owner fit him well. Joe's father had passed on significant land holdings which he managed well and increased in size.

Joe had lost an eye from catching birdshot in it while he was trying to shoot a dog that had killed his sheep. Sneaking up to the man's house at night to shoot the canine, Joe failed to consider that the dog's owner could have expected company and anticipated firing the first shot. Men dealing with the realities of life as they felt appropriate could confront harsh consequences.

Coming from a family of nine, Daddy had thin indigenous roots with only a sister nearby who lived in Iron City with her husband and family. The sister and spouse had two sons and two daughters whose families lived near Iron City, except for one who had moved out of state. Daddy's other siblings had relocated to Tallahassee, Jacksonville or South Florida before my birth which explains the shortage of resident Mills relatives in comparison to the Spooners and Trawicks.

The introduction of new labor saving equipment, chiefly tractors, resulted in an ongoing migration from the farms to the cities and caused farmers to have smaller broods

CHAPTER 2

HAPPENINGS AND INFLUENCES

When reaching the retirement years, seniors can best look back and assess their lives and what they did or did not do with their time on the planet. Retrospectively, older folks cherish the exhilarating times and cringe at the unpleasant and wonder why their own one-person "brain trusts" made those exceedingly stupid blunders. A finite number of relationships, occurrences and conditions shape people's lives and create the person whom relations recognize. Of course, who that person becomes can only be a myopic view that is inaccurate by anyone's measure. Others assess us along the way, but with views that range widely and no way to document, analyze and learn from the varied opinions.

My goal is to dig deeply into life to better understand the "who and why" of my composition because I am not so naïve as to strive for a full understanding. The stories that I share relate occurrences which I regarded as significant in recall and should provide insights and explanations. To reflect accurately on life requires a level of honesty which I could find painful at times. But, I truly believe what Mama always said, "Honesty is the best policy."

At age three I remember an instance with Mama on our front porch. Mama offered a breast which seemed appropriate since it had been a chief source of nourishment. She pulled it out of her bosom and asked if I wanted it, an act that had transpired routinely in my tender years. Why was Mama offering it? Was I continuing to breast feed at that age? Being her last child, I can guess Mama preferred temporarily to maintain that part of life and the nurturing relationship we had. Twins, who Mama birthed about a year after me and had died at delivery, could explain the supply of milk and the need to nurse. Could she remain affected by the loss? That recollection, along with the many other motherly kindnesses, kept us close as I grew up.

When Daddy had reached the maximum alcohol buzz on Saturday nights, he would pull me onto his lap, tickle my ribs and call me his little pig. This interaction brought laughs and wiggles but Daddy's attention came only when he drank booze. Mama provided the touches, the hugs and the tenderness seven days a week with no starting and stopping of the flow.

While walking alone in a pasture adjacent to the house, I silently stated, "I am four years old." The memory, nesting so well in the cranium for these long years, seemed odd. Since no one accompanied me, this young recollection could have represented a rudimentary attempt at breaking away and struggling with a beginning level of independence as I started to formulate an identity.

At four or five years old, my parents obtained a pit bull puppy that Mama named Dash. He became a loyal companion, my only playmate and protector for six years. Dash could catch rabbits, dig rats out of holes and crack pecans for me, who did not understand that dog slobber possibly could be viewed as nasty. The pecan tree produced a Money Maker variety of armored nuts which could only be cracked with a hammer or Dash's strong jaws, so squirrels could often be seen carrying a tiny hammer to save their teeth from the thick, unwieldy shells.

The fateful day that I first experienced something shocking, Dash and I had trekked across land adjacent to our farm when two thin wires strung between posts obstructed our path. The wires appeared to form a fence but my brain responded, "Such a flimsy wire would not stop farm animals and certainly could not stop us." Laying my BB gun on the ground and grabbing a wire with each hand to pull them apart to provide space to step through, brought a big jolt. As I grasped both at the same time, the shaking of my life occurred which resulted in a flash trip to the ground and me gasping for breath. Dash, dog-wary with senses so keen he could smell electricity, had a pit bull snicker and a smile on his face, but in recognition of my "man down" predicament, he muffled a loud laugh. Depositing the encounter in my brain bank, I solemnly made a pledge to self, "Self, steer clear of thin wires."

Having no same age children to play with taxed my "pretend" creativity. The closest brother Jerome who was six and a half years older offered no help in the playing department since he specialized in torture. Lacking other alternatives, I learned to play alone and to use imagination for inventing playmates. Playing Roy Rogers and chasing the bad men with two toy guns and a holster came to be my favorite act. One roll of "caps" came with the pistols at Christmas so when the ammo ran out, pretending the gun made a bang had to suffice.

Jerome, my worst nightmare, held the claim to "baby" until my birth, unbeknownst to me when I exited the womb. Patricia, whom we called Sister, and my brother Lloyd both commented, "Jerome was bothered when Mama first brought you into the house." He did not want to have interactions with the baby and preferred by actions and words that I magically vanish. Sister and Lloyd related that Jerome told Mama, "You have your baby now," and never accepted the new infant in the house. The simple act of bringing a newborn into the house created an insurmountable wall which prevented Jerome and me from having a brotherly relationship or even a sensible conversation.

This introduction into the family had such a huge effect on my life and Jerome's that I wondered how our lives could have been different if Mama had found the "switch" she could have flicked to keep Jerome in balance. Perhaps if Mama had said the right words and given the right hugs at the right time, Jerome and I could have had a productive relationship. I had to eventually put the disappointment in a file of "that's the way it is" and accept the relationship.

At my age four, Jerome began his harassment, easily riling me with his huge age and size superiority. Regardless of the antagonism, a kid wants to look up to big brother, so I kept returning for mistreatment.

The family had a "some of this and some of that" collection of dinnerware including a spoon, shinier than the rest, which came to be a source of aggravation and competition. Jerome called it the shiniest spoon in the world in order to cause me to want it. Then, he tried to ensure that only he used it at the table. Compared to Jerome's eventual repertoire of ways to torture, this aggravation I would label as a minor annoyance.

A tremendous contrast existed between the relationship of conflict with Jerome and the loving, caring, normal relationships with Lloyd and Sister, nine and ten years older, respectively. Sister took care of me in my baby days to take a load off Mama which resulted in our having a special relationship. Sister related, "I thought I would grow crooked from carrying you on my hip." Lloyd bought my first BB gun, twenty-two rifle and shotgun which perpetuated hero worship and contrasted Jerome's meting out of a rough time in Mama's absence.

Sister accidentally put me in a life-threatening predicament at the age of four when Mama asked her to give me an aspirin. She opened the tin of aspirin, placed them on the edge of a table and became distracted. In a brief period, Mama noticed the empty tin and asked what had happened to the aspirin, the question bringing my response, "They tasted good."

Daddy, Mama and I rode to the hospital to visit Dr. Baxley for stomach pumping and instructions for Mama to keep me awake for hours. Mama sat on the edge of the bed throughout the night and occasionally prodded me to prevent total sleep. Similar occurrences cemented the deep love I had for Mama who returned it in spades, unconditionally until her passing.

Mama and Daddy would visit relatives on nights or Sunday afternoons leaving Jerome and me home, presenting a time for him to hand out unmitigated torture. I was too naive to suspect what was to happen when Mama and Daddy departed. But the script of mistreatments started again including locking me out of the house in the dark, holding me down while sitting on my chest and chasing, with me realizing when Jerome caught me, he could do whatever he wished. Locking me outside at night when I was five years old became one of Jerome's favorites because he had determined the dark horrified me. Only after my screaming and frantic banging on the door did he open it, flashing that smile and laugh, indicating what a kick he had received from the mistreatment.

When I became older and could run faster, Jerome had a harder time catching me to do the dirt. Once after interrupting my shower behind the smokehouse, he initiated a chase which caused me to run naked down the road hoping cars would pass. Limited vehicles traveled on the dirt road in the '50s, or I would have truly freaked when startled drivers swerved in the road and probably laughed.

When Mama came home, I would tell on Jerome, and he would suffer a switching if the cruelty was deemed to be abusive. This punishment, triggered by me, inflamed Jerome who exacted his revenge the next time we stayed home together. Learning from these encounters, I became unlikely to relate the mistreatments to Mama and realized Jerome and I would never have a normal relationship. Tolerating a bad predicament seemed the best choice.

The major factors of Mama's love, Daddy's drinking, the lack of playmates on the farm, poverty and an abusive sibling molded my personality and mindset during the formative years. Daddy's alcohol habit and Jerome's abuse, I would select as the chief negatives which created insecurities I would one day have to overcome to better wrap my arms around life.

Seldom do people come through their young lives without emotional scars. They may or may not resolve the deep injuries before reaching adulthood and becoming capable of creating a reasonably accurate perspective of what happened and why.

CHAPTER 3
THE HOUSE

The family lived in a five room sharecropper house, built circa 1920, containing about 1000 square feet of space, without a speck of paint. At least four sharecropper houses were down the road near our house with all having the same floor plan and construction type. Our abode consisted of a full bedroom, a combination bedroom-sitting room, a combination bedroom-living room, a dining room which was a bedroom until the older kids left home, a fireplace and a kitchen.

A water pipe came through the wall in the kitchen with a water bucket and dipper which sat beneath the faucet. With the prevailing ignorance of germs, everyone including relatives who visited used the dipper.

A five gallon slop bucket for depositing table scraps which we fed to the pigs occupied a corner of the kitchen and was an eternal main attraction for houseflies. During cold nights, the males of our family would pee in the bucket, aware the pigs liked whatever it contained, and on warmer nights we urinated while standing on the edge of the back porch with no concern for who might be in the dark.

A faucet, pan and washstand on the back porch we used for washing hands and faces when we came in after work or for that wake-up face splash in the mornings. The household possessed all the comforts of the time for those in our station in life.

Mama basked in the luxury of a "slop jar" (chamber pot) which sat by her bed for her toilet needs. It had a lid which contained the smells until the user removed it; then, we would look out for an odor that would peel paint off the walls if there had been any.

Located roughly fifty yards behind the house was a two-holer outhouse, complete with a functioning Sears catalog. Considering everyone's habit of performing the daily constitutional alone, I wondered of the purpose of the second hole, but Mama surprisingly joined me once at an irregular time during which she gave a lesson on how to rub the catalog paper together and crunch it to create a soft, pliable "tissue." This lesson exemplifies how the family used time wisely by making "toilet paper" while perching on the "throne."

In the summer season, the males and occasionally Mama, took showers behind the smokehouse where a Clabber Girl baking powder can with ice pick holes in its bottom hung from a rafter. A water hose inserted in the top of the can produced the convenience of a cold shower with a temperature of whatever the water possessed when it traveled through the pipe. After returning from work late in the day, the sensation of water running down our backs and faces invigorated and relaxed tired bodies. The water came at a comfortable temperature until the pump kicked in and started pumping colder water from deep in the ground bringing a chill when the cold first hit which always made the spine stiffen.

Throughout my first seventeen years on this earth, I had undergone having only a cold water faucet in the house, a reality which produced a continuing appreciation for the convenience of choosing water temperature after I became an adult.

Come the late fall, winter and early spring, the family used a #2 galvanized washtub for bathing which held five to ten gallons of water brought to a comfortable temperature by heating it on the stove. After we entered the tub and sat down, we could not avoid biting lips when leaning back against the cold side.

The front porch had a sizeable wood framed shaving mirror hanging on the wall and a faucet nearby with a wash stand where I saw Daddy shave when I was young. A friend of Granddaddy's had carved the mirror frame out of a soft wood with a pocket knife, and Granddaddy had used it daily for years. Four or five rocking chairs and a swing comprised the remainder of the front porch furnishings. On Sunday afternoons Mama and Daddy sat in the rocking chairs, talked and watched the cars pass while the children occupied the swing which offered the joy of floating back and forth.

Having savored the refinements of the time which came with being on the lower end of the financial stratum, hearing kids at school speaking of having "a room" sounded novel since I had only known communal sharing. These instances separated me from others who had hugely contrasting experiences in childhood.

The old outer boards of the house, porous and weathered with daylight peeking through in spots, especially on the west side where strong winds would drive rain water through the walls, allowed water to drip in the edge of rooms. Mama always became worried about her homemade curtains and would pull them away from the leaky windows in an attempt to prevent wetting.

In midsummer Mama would sit down with the latest Sears catalog, which had not made it to the outhouse, to choose pairs of shoes, pants and shirts for the boys to wear, complete the order form and enclose it with a check in an envelope. Work clothes for Daddy plus items for her and sister, Mama selected from this best source of affordable wear, and several weeks afterward the clothes arrived making us the proud and spiffy owners of new outfits.

I always flipped through the older edition "dream book" while visiting "Miss Murphy" and imagined having the toys, bicycles and other children's treasures. Montgomery Wards' catalog, Sears only competition, which probably did not meet Mama's standard for toilet paper, never found use in our "palace."

By the age of twelve, through observations and thoughtful reasoning I had determined that the family had a well-below-standard existence and became bothered by the house and its lack of creature comforts. With an innate yearning for our furnishings to parallel other families', I felt differentiated from the bulk of my friends who had better, better everything. Did we somehow not make the cut and fall into a different category of well-being? At the time, I thought families who lived in painted houses with a bathroom must be rich, knowing those accoutrements to be a distant possibility for us.

Perhaps unknowingly a few people responded in an uncomplimentary way to us and our lifestyle — relatives. There were the vast bulk of kinfolks who treated us as equals without regard for our financial well-being. However, there was a small minority who ignored us and essentially pretended that we did not exist. But with the Grace of God, I have been able to forgive them and regard their actions as what they could not help but feel in their hearts at the time. It had to be a learned behavior since they could not have come into the world feeling that way.

Making a point of inviting only a select number of friends to visit, kids would put me in a situation where I could not refuse. How could I tell a friend who needed help with homework that he cannot come to the house? Our domicile had become a source of embarrassment, and I would make no apologies for the mindset, though I tried to keep it from Mama and Daddy. A first cousin Jimmy Williams spent the night at the house numerous times; his being a member of the family made it acceptable to have him around and I not feel inadequate.

Filing income taxes for the first time circa 1960, Daddy said that within the tax guidelines he never had enough income to report. Not earning over $600 per year to that point, he was exempt. His reason for filing was to pay sufficient "quarters," so he could draw social security when turning sixty-five.

Living in the old sharecropper shack, the family had a roof over its head and I had a place to call home for the first eighteen years of my life, but the domicile did not hold a warm spot in my heart. However, the family who lived there continues to provide a sense of belonging and of being a part of something significant. In retrospect, I can only view the house as a monument to Daddy's lack of ambition.

CHAPTER 4
RESPONSIBILITIES

Daddy sharecropped peanuts and corn with relatives, farming about fifty acres of sharecrop land plus our fifty, which produced sufficient work to keep me busy before school, after school and during the summers.

City school friends called it summer vacation, but the word never entered my thoughts because three months of long twelve hour days, with caring for animals, tending the crops and the harvesting, constituted no "escape."

Before I was six years of age, Daddy assigned the easier tasks, prepping me for the challenging work to come as I grew. The progression started with bringing in wood, which had been cut and stacked in the barnyard by Daddy and my brothers, and stacking it by the fireplace.

Oak produced a longer, hotter fire but was tough to chop and not always available. A crosscut saw could be used to effectively cut the hardwoods. As Daddy did not own one, he periodically borrowed from a neighbor. Kindling for starting the fires, which I had to splinter off with an ax, came from pine stumps rich in resin or pine tar.

At times my child's brain operated as a source of extreme dismay for me and any innocent bystanders. About my age of five, Jerome carried a load of wood in his arms, as nearby I played cowboys with action racing in my psyche to fit the play. At the Donalsonville theatre, I had seen the man with the white hat hit the villain over the head with a pistol often.

Somehow Jerome's presence and the animosity between us played into the brain and my cowboy thing, resulting in my cracking him on the head with the toy pistol. To my amazement Jerome dropped the wood and started crying, not doing the passing out thing the bad guys performed so well.

Mama, having heard the commotion from the kitchen, came out for a re-enactment of the switch dance to whatever beat I preferred. Repeating the performance of the last time Mama used the limb, and I ran in one spot while she held my arm and flailed away motivating me to keep fantasy and reality separated and obliterating any potential thoughts of whacking the bad brother on the head.

Similar to other farm families, we consumed a quantity of milk and butter, so two milk cows pastured every day in the woods behind our farm on land we did not own but had permission to use for grazing. The older brothers herded the cows a quarter mile to the woods each morning after milking them and from the woods each evening to milk them.

Having reduced to one cow as siblings left home, at my age twelve, Daddy assigned me the task of milking Butterfly. Draining the cow mornings and evenings developed a fine grip for handshaking, an accomplishment which I would find helpful in my future business life.

Butterfly always swung her tail to swat at flies and tossed trash with the motion, a habit which caused me to watch for it and the debris associated to keep the milk as clean as possible. Being a belligerent bovine, the cow periodically would slap me on the head for kicks. If debris flew into the milk, Mama removed it by straining with cheesecloth into a pan before storing it in the refrigerator.

Daddy dearly loved "Blue John" (skimmed milk); therefore, he would be seen in the fridge a couple of times a day blowing back the cream on top, turning the pan up and having a drink. When finished, Daddy would have clabber on the top lip which he wiped away with a hand or shirt sleeve. Having observed this routine often, I had no intention of picking up the habit and chose to have my dairy in a glass or as butter.

As the pans of milk rested in the cooler, the cream would rise to the top so Mama could skim it into a churn for accumulating a sufficient amount for churning butter. When I was seven or eight years old, Mama gave notice that the time had come for me to churn butter. She pulled out a chair, put the churn in my lap, cranked the handle several turns to demonstrate the speed and said, "Go to work." She offered a suggestion, "Saying the words, come butter come, come butter come, over and over again will cause the butter to form faster." Mama had, figuratively speaking, grabbed my leg and given it a big yank. After cranking awhile, I felt compelled to try the words out of desperation owing to boredom and a longing to play outside. It made no difference.

Surprisingly, the butter would gather fast sometimes, but other times I cranked seemingly forever. When butter began to gather, the crank would become stiff as I turned it, and a big ball, having a deep shade of yellow which shoppers do not see today, was visible through the glass. Mama packed the butter into a rectangular mold, let it set for a while in the fridge to firm up, and with the mold handle pushed the yellow cube out of the mold onto a dish to complete the process.

Butter, hot biscuits and cane syrup made a powerful combination at breakfast. Being a huge ingredient in nourishing the family, Mama used butter in baking cakes, pies and other confections and as grease in the pan for frying eggs. When Daddy's out of state relatives visited, they would request butter to carry back.

Taking advantage of Daddy's accommodating nature at times, relatives would ask for a slab of bacon or a ham which displayed lack of sensitivity to our family's financial position. Daddy had a hard time saying no to his "better off" brothers and sisters.

Daddy always had about thirty swine including three-six brood sows. The rest were slaughtered for the table or sold at the market when they reached top weight. In the winter time, when funds were low, the hogs could be a source of needed cash.

Mornings and evenings we fed the hogs corn and dumped the slop bucket from the kitchen into the trough, which they usually fought over, being drawn by the strong smell and their warped taste buds. Swine would eat about anything including chickens that came inside the pig pen, but they miraculously assimilated that unpleasant stuff into tasty pork.

Betty, a Poland China brood sow, when being protective of young piglets, could assume an offensive posture causing me to use caution and avoid being bitten. Picking up on nature, the devil inside me would insist that I irritate her by squealing like a pig. Betty would always give serious ten yard chases which I found entertaining and challenging.

Along came the day when Betty changed the game without notice as I performed the fake squeal routine. Betty came charging and I started running while looking back over a shoulder, anticipating her slowing and stopping. Noticing that Betty's pursuit had gone to a new, longer distance and a faster pace, I turned on the afterburners and shifted to a faster gear with her close behind and running wide open. Rapidly, I picked up the pace and raced for a fence which I piled over as she ran into it. That ended the pestering of Betty with me aware that if we had a biting contest, she would take away the prize, one of my legs or worse.

Learning to shoulder responsibilities at a young age prepared me for a better run at life. In fact, in a few important endeavors I have been too responsible which can put stress on a man. The valued lessons from Mama and Daddy sustained and helped me experience a better, more productive life.

CHAPTER 5

MAMA AND DADDY

Children loathe heart damaging conflict between parents and prefer to have the two they love to live in harmony. When I was five or six years of age, Mama and Daddy had a loud quarrel playing out a continuing drama precipitated by bouts of drunkenness. Daddy would start drinking Saturday afternoon in town, come home and keep drinking, causing Mama to filch and hide the bottle whenever possible.

Wanting additional booze, Daddy planned to head to the liquor store, but Mama would find a way to thwart the trip by snitching the truck keys. Denying a drunk access to his hemlock causes anger, so Daddy would become belligerent and seek whatever measures available to travel to the liquor store. Daddy's nature dictated that he should not strike Mama causing a quest for leverage through other avenues.

One Saturday night at my age of five, I lay in bed, awakened by yelling, and determined Daddy had become angry, shouting that he would bang up the truck with an ax he had in his hand, if Mama did not give up the keys. Sensing helplessness, I became extremely disturbed because the quarrel imposed a conflict of loyalties between the two I loved dearly. If the ax erroneously struck either one, I would be horrified realizing it could bring traumatic damage.

This quandary of helplessness and fear added to the mental scar tissue from other altercations and resumed the etching of an irremovable trench in my brain. While lying in bed with indescribable fear, I felt overcome with strong sensations of insecurity which remained long after the night ended. The frightening event had similarities to the fear Jerome had invoked repeatedly.

Unwavering, Mama dominated and Daddy did not drive away in the truck. The next morning, with apprehension, I checked for damage to the vehicle and discovered no ax dents.

A weekend alcoholic, Daddy vacillated between difficult to handle and gentle as a puppy dog. In instances when Mama had secured the truck keys, Daddy might walk to the road and flag down a friend or relative to hitchhike a ride dependent on how badly he needed the next swig and the lateness of the evening. As Daddy rode away, we wondered when the family would see him again. He would usually return that night or on Sunday with a ride from a drinking buddy.

To reconcile his behaviors, he rationalized that five days of hard work had earned him the manly right to a drink on Saturday. Ninety-five percent plus of instances found him sober on Sunday morning and ready to work on Monday. It was the other occasions that scared Mama and me terribly.

About five times Daddy tied on an extreme bender while having the vehicle and was missing for two or three days. After one sojourn, I saw him vomiting blood, probably from terrible stomach abuse. During those rough days, I could read the weight of worry on Mama's face that affected me as well wishing so desperately that Daddy's truck motor would be heard as he pulled into the driveway. At the center of my fears was, "What would happen to us without Daddy?"

One Saturday night Daddy made Mama mad, motivating her to strike him powerfully with a broom, and the lick dropped him like a rock. She bent over him to check for injuries. Playing possum, Daddy erupted in a loud laugh inspiring Mama to grab the broom and whop him again displaying toughness of which she had a bounty.

If Daddy had the keys and wanted liquor, Mama would send along an older child, counting on him returning in consideration of the kid's safety. An observer could question the logic, but serious car wrecks did not happen often in the '50s. Once accompanied by Sister, Daddy drove the old Ford into a ditch while traveling up the hill west from Rock Pond. The unpaved road had deep ditches of red clay from rain washing down the hill that produced a risk for anyone to slide in if not driving straight. Sister walked the half mile to the house alone in the night leaving Daddy to handle the problem.

In actuality Daddy's drinking contributed heavily to the family not owning but fifty acres of land and living a sharecropper family's life. Mama often told him, "You cannot see past the end of your nose," which indicated Daddy would not take on the burden and risk of purchasing additional acreage. Being stuck in time and having no ambition to improve our lot in life, Daddy preferred living in the house Granddaddy Mills lived in, getting drunk on Saturdays and playing his guitar and mandolin when friends held a get-together.

A far cry from the father figures on TV, Daddy avoided closeness to me. Working together extensively, he would offer an occasional comment on the weather or work, but we had no conversations. For an unknown reason, Daddy lacked motivation to do father-son hunting or fishing other than when Mama quietly insisted. Counsel on what to do with my life came through Mama's gentle urgings to pursue an education as Daddy offered no advice.

Not once did he lay a hand on me in anger, but I always did what Daddy asked. His orders I viewed as a command to do the given task, always respecting him completely from a work standpoint since Daddy had strong commitment and put in long hours. Thankfully, he taught me how to work which was a valuable lesson to learn for my future.

Given the circumstances of my young life, playing alone and having a daddy who did not communicate well, reticence in relationships could have been expected. At my age fourteen, Daddy and I had stopped at great Uncle Gordon Spooner's store for a cold drink, a visit which occurred regularly. Having noticed the presence of others in the store and my silence, as he drove down the road Daddy said, "Son, why do you not talk to people? You never say anything," words that created a brain stretching realization which attached firmly in my brain. Daddy and I had stopped there often, and I had never been the life of the party. Why did his expectations suddenly change?

About the age of fifteen, I complained to Daddy regarding work he wanted to do, hoeing fence rows. Having a logical, questioning nature, I could not understand the reason for chopping the weeds and other foliage along a fence since the vegetation would grow back and require chopping next year. The tradition of helping his father hoe fence rows apparently had given Daddy blindness to questioning the work.

Usually even tempered, he must have had worries since he snapped, "Son, you are never going to amount to anything." In a poor response to the questioning of the work, he had condemned my future life. Unaware of the effect of those words, Daddy had applied the best motivator I would ever have and had spontaneously instilled a strong want to prove him wrong and make Mama proud.

In contrast Mama possessed a strong backbone for standing firm and communicating effectively, unknowingly teaching social skills through example. Mama would spend quality time teaching me to write my name in cursive before I started school. Mama's stories of siblings and life with her parents brought yesteryear to life whetting my appetite for tales of old. Accounts of walking two miles to school as a child with sisters carrying lunch in a syrup bucket and having a hot sweet potato in her pocket in the winter to keep her hands warm, I loved.

In a handful of times, witnessing her sadness, Mama's plight gave a giant yank to my heart strings. On a Thanksgiving when no siblings made it home, Mama shed tears and could not understand the absence, displaying the deep love a mother possesses for those to whom she gave life and her huge disappointment when that love seemingly was not returned

CHAPTER 6

A BAD DAY AT MILLS HOTEL

"Spooner Town, Trawick Street, Mills Hotel and not a damn thing to eat," so went a saying commonly heard in our family. It always brought a laugh and had shades of truth in its.

In the winter of 1950, Grandmother Chloe Trawick lay on her death bed at our house. Frequently, the terminally ill died at home for personal, family, privacy or financial reasons. A serious tone permeated the house, but at five years old I could not understand the depth of what was transpiring.

As in any other winter, nature set about its work as usual on the farm. In a barn stall, one of Daddy's sow's had a litter of pigs with the "runt" having a slim possibility of living. Daddy mentioned the piglet to Mama, and she chose to cheat the natural order. She removed the piglet from the litter being mindful that the sow usually crushed runts because their size and weakness prevented them from staying out of the way when she lay down to nurse. With a baby bottle, Mama saved the tiny pig's life and gave him the name Pinky, a name suggested by the white Landrace breed and young age which caused him to have a pink hue.

Pinky thrived and became a healthy animal with the run of the yard and constantly followed family members around like a magnet. Frolicking and scampering with Dash, Pinky was a delight to watch by the family and relatives who visited.

A nightmare with the pig approached, a deed which would put me in bad graces with the family with only my youth saving me from a tossing off the Brinson Bridge in a crocus sack. The event explained why I entered the first grade before I figured out my last name was not Brains, and the first, not Shifer.

With me playing outside, the toy of the day, an old three-pronged, broken-handled pitchfork which made it easy to handle became an unintended weapon. The play activity involved tossing the fork into the air and watching it stick in the ground when it came down.

With Pinky scampering nearby, I gave the fork a strong toss, but he happened to stand where it came down. One prong of the fork entered Pinky's back quadrant, the internal organs. Pinky let out a squeal so loud the ladies heard it inside, bringing Mama running out the back door to hover over Pinky and remove the pitchfork. She picked him up and presented me with a look that could crack concrete. With me trying to swallow a lump in the back of my throat, my brain proclaimed, "You have really done it this time."

Mama jumped into the car with Pinky and raced off to town leaving me with a cold, impenetrable wall created by the women caring for Grandmother. For this heinous act, I should pay dearly because Pinky had become a cherished part of the family. I dreaded Mama's return, realizing an execution, or worse, could be in the offing since I had a debt to pay.

Mama could not find Dr. Davis, the veterinarian, so she took Pinky to Dr. Baxley who pronounced the darling piglet beyond recovery and near death. The one and only office visit for a swine in his career cemented an esteemed standing for the doctor in the community, and piggy heaven received another piglet angel.

When Mama returned, she did not bother with the ritual of me breaking a peach tree limb which she selected. Her need to administer justice quickly changed protocol with me suspecting that a trip to a guillotine would have been better than the impending switching. She broke a limb, shredded the leaves and dispensed a truckload of pain.

With instances of mischievousness in the past, Mama would say, "Your britches will not hold shucks when I finish with you." After completing the "whuppin'," Mama could have dropped shucks in the top back of my overalls, and they would have fallen through to the ankles as if lead. The caboose had about disappeared, so the old expression could hold true, "It would take nine cats to catch a rat in the seat of my pants."

Mama buried Pinky in the back yard, probably with "words." Conspicuously, she offered me no invite to the funeral to pay respects and voice regrets.

Why Pinky did not visit the table with an apple in his mouth, considering the importance of food, stirred my curiosity. Asking Mama regarding Pinky's disposal, would only cause antagonism of which I had exceeded my daily allowance. At a tender age, I had learned to watch for occurrences when silence should drive the prudence wagon.

What a traumatic day! The recollection was locked in my brain with a steel padlock, so I felt fated to carry the death of Pinky to the grave.

When similar mishaps emerged in the future, I would eventually gain the know-how and acumen to handle what landed on my porch. Life's quirks, disappointments and struggles would continue the rest of my life as it happens with everyone.

CHAPTER 7
THE SHOW

The building with the huge screen, sound and moving pictures, locals did not call the theatre or the movie house, instead referring to The Dunn Theatre's auditorium with people alive on the screen as "the show."

My initial exposure came at five years old with Mama informing us of a reward trip to the show in the afternoon after we cleaned the barnyard. With her shouting orders, we four went to work, excited to see a show which was a major event in our lives. Little help came from my actions, but by focusing here and there, I made a small contribution with Dash, my constant interruption, tagging along. We collected, piled, burned and hoed until the barnyard looked as if a sandy desert.

Besides the clean appearance, the barren yard made it easier to spot the chicken poop, so we could avoid stepping in it in the summer when we wore no shoes. Going barefoot, always had the risk of chicken manure squirting between our toes with the messiness requiring a trip to a faucet for a foot bath.

Late in the afternoon, we loaded into the old Ford and rattled off to the show, excited of seeing the movie entitled "I Would Climb the

Highest Mountain" starring William Lundigan as a Methodist minister and Susan Hayward as his wife. By today's standards the movie would not draw three patrons, but at the time any show became special entertainment with the theatre crowded as usual. We delighted in our well-earned reward which was a benchmark for me since it was my first-remembered movie.

The outing whetted my appetite for shows, so on Saturdays when the family went to town to purchase groceries, I headed for the theatre. Roy Rogers, Gene Autry, Rocky Lane, Durango Kid, Red Ryder and Little Beaver, Rex Allen, Gabby Hayes, Smiley Burnette and others brought the Old West to life. The guys with the white hats fought the guys in the black hats with Roy's and Gene's shows providing time for them to sing boring songs; action had brought me to the show, not music. The good guys, killing hundreds of bad men, or so it appeared, left me wondering why they would appear in movies with such a high risk of meeting their maker.

The serials and cartoons provided a warm-up for the action movie to follow with Elmer Fudd, Bugs Bunny, Wiley Coyote and Woody Woodpecker making the kids laugh. Action serials completed the pre-movie offering; some serials starred Johnny Weismuller and Buster Crabbe in jungle-themed adventures which continued the following Saturday. Rocket Man had a suit that propelled him through the air to chase the villains. When he would tune the buttons on the front of the suit to gain acceleration, I was thrilled, understanding that Rocket Man would save the day for those facing a menace. At the end of every segment, he confronted a life threatening predicament of peril, but the audience rested assured that on the next Saturday, he would narrowly avoid the clutch of doom.

The only one that I can remember selling the ten cent admission tickets was Miss Beatrice, a serious, older, gray haired lady who helped with the drinks, popcorn and the world's best hot dogs. When I received an extra dime, the best dog with its unique relish became my treat of choice.

The management had jackpot night on Tuesdays, an attraction which brought in larger audiences if the jackpot surpassed one hundred dollars. The patrons anxiously held onto their ticket stubs until after the show when Bob McLeod would draw a number on stage, and an excited, lucky person received the cash prize.

On one Tuesday night, Mama placed her shoes in a diaper's contents which a thoughtless mother had deposited on the floor. If Mama had known who had done it, fur would have flown. Only brief mutterings left her mouth on the way home. A festering within her caused me to table question-asking until an amenable demeanor prevailed.

I would visit the Dunn Theater with its Old West offerings, and Lloyd, Jerome and Sister would patronize the People's Theatre which played the adult, mostly war, movies since WWII had ended only several years previously.

On a rare occasion, Jerome accompanied me to the Dunn Theater, and he sat by Dewayne Roberts who asked if he would be her boyfriend. The transaction happened so casually I imagined the ease with which I could one day find girlfriends. What a shock, to the contrary. Attracting the opposite sex had its challenges, as I later learned so well.

Mama and Daddy would drop me at the show and suggest a general area where they intended to park the car. On the surface it appeared to be a workable plan, but it had an aggravating flaw. A limited capability of predicting a car parking spot because of full parking spaces on Saturday afternoons sometimes made locating the Ford difficult.

When unable to find the vehicle, I became frantic. Separation from Mama brought desperation. I would walk the streets plowing through the waves of humanity to search for her. With hundreds of folks populating the downtown streets, doing their shopping and visiting, the task of finding Mama was unwieldy for a six year old. If I did not find her soon, plan B involved crying my eyes out with my pitiful tears bringing forth the women who would try consolation.

But only Mama possessed the magic required to stop the blubbering. Eventually a "comforter" would run into Mama, describe my sad demeanor and give her an approximate location. What a relief when Mama gave me that warm hug!

CHAPTER 8

IRON CITY SCHOOL

With trepidation I entered the first grade at Iron City Elementary School in September 1950: What a huge life changer! The first day at school felt as if I had mentally landed on another planet in a faraway galaxy. Giving up Mama and Dash, my closest friends, I had to adjust to my new surroundings and classmates. Having no playmates on the farm, I had developed minimum social skills, a deficit which initially caused difficulty with assimilating this strange, new, fearful world and its inhabitants.

My teacher Johnnie Martin jolted my psyche with her two moods: stern and dead serious. I determined that her demeanor communicated "legitimate threat" and suspected that she could inflict bodily harm at the arch of an eyebrow. Just weeks down the road, she confirmed my suspicions big time.

Soon the class started traveling with Alice and Jerry and their parents in a travel trailer akin to an Airstream which they used to explore the country and have educational adventures. "See Alice run, See Jerry run, See Jip run," comprised the content. With my intellect the first reader attraction ended fast and soon became boring.

Training us to recognize our names, our teacher had cards with our names written on them that she would hold up in front of the class. That exercise became old quicker than Alice and Jerry though the lesson did help us to start learning the alphabet. To introduce the class to numbers, the teacher used cards showing two numbers and the total. She would cover the sum, and the students had to say aloud the answer.

In order to expose us to a broad range of subjects, a coloring class was offered. God gave me no artistic talent, but He provided other blessings. I hated coloring. We used our Crayola crayons to color pictures on construction paper with a borderline sandpaper texture, the worst excuse for coloring material. With my level of expertise, it probably did not matter which medium I used when working at the tables in the back of the room which gave students a roomy, flat surface for art work.

After coloring class, Miss Martin instructed the students to walk orderly back to their desks. Since Joseph Cross and I competed at everything, we would race at every opportunity, so one day we raced back to our desks. The lion tamer disapproved emphatically of our antics, so she pulled out her paddle and gave both of us whacks. What a shocker! She hurt both my butt and my ego. The surprise consequences left me crying from the pain and the embarrassment in front of my peers.

Only Mama had burned my bottom until then, so I was convinced this woman carried a measure of authority. Apparently Miss Martin did not want spontaneity in her class, so this feedback to my lower half was noted, and I avoided future chastisement and ridicule.

To keep the potbellied coal heater replenished with fuel in the winter, Miss Martin assigned the rotating job of filling up the coal box during lunch period to Joseph and me. On the assigned day, we had other priorities because visiting the coal pile behind the lunchroom had evaporated from our brains. The following lunch we basked in the presence and glory of our loving teacher including a direct trip back to the room with her when we had finished our meals. This point of doing what the schoolmarm asked started to gain a grip on the brain.

Two cute girls, whose names will remain anonymous to protect the guilty, became my first source of female distress which every male is bound to experience eventually. They encouraged our first attempts at puppy love, and in a handful of instances, we gave them a kiss on the cheek. Having been led by the nose, sweet Joseph and I would have never initiated such folderol. Luckily, the teacher did not witness the cheek pecking, or we would have spent time hanging by our toes or worse.

The difficulty came from my brother Jerome who had learned of the kissing and had used it as leverage to divert Mama's attention when he had broken one of her rules. Judging from Mama's anger, she must have figured that we had plans to elope and run away. So again the time came to visit the peach tree and break off a limb of Mama's choosing. "Molesting" the opposite sex had lost its attraction.

Our principal Monk Stein, with a glass eye, may have cast a foreboding look our way, but he could mitigate it with his smile. Comfortable in his role among the children, Mr. Stein often was seen playing ball with them, a routine which supported his style of ruling with quiet authority and respect.

Goosey, a popular game which we played before school each day when there was no rain, pulled in a substantial participation. In the school yard adjacent to the class rooms, we played the game where the players tried to run from one end of the school building to the other without being caught by the students who had already been "goosed." Increasingly, kids were caught and had to chase, so it became progressively more difficult to pass through to the other end.

Marbles became my first exposure at putting a treasure at risk. The game began with a circle etched on the ground in which the players placed marbles in the center. Shooting from the edge of the circle with our favorite marble, we tried to knock marbles out of the ring. A player kept shooting until he did not knock one out, his miss providing an opening for the next person in order to have his turn. The kids became owners of the marbles they shot from the ring. Therefore a player had the possibility to win or lose marbles. Kids would often cry when they lost their marbles which occasionally resulted in a "softie" giving them back to stop the blubbering.

One afternoon after boarding the school to take us home, I gazed out the window. Squared off at the southwest corner of the building, under an old cedar tree, were my brother Jerome and our cousin Will Trawick slugging it out and spewing foul words. Their cursing far exceeded the slugging. Jerome missing the bus held my innocent concern, but luckily they ended the altercation and boarded the ride in time, or the driver Buck Sharber would have probably left them.

An entertaining activity involved girls in the seventh grade whom first grade boys would pick at to cause a chase with the caught kids getting tickled. June Hornsby and Dewayne Roberts, plus other seventh grade girls, ran after us and had as much fun as we did. A striking beauty, June held the honor of being the first older female I regarded as pretty, a recognition which caused a slower pace on my part when she ran after me.

My two-years-older cousin Richard Trawick was notorious as a rambunctious kid on the school grounds. He was not just rowdy but rowdy to the power of infinity. Occupying a major portion of his time out of the classroom, his favorite joys in life were wrestling and fighting. Traveling from brawl to brawl during lunch and recess, Richard scraped incessantly with his salty language adding new words to my vocabulary. When at home, I had to be careful and avoid using the words around Mama since she did not even allow "dang" which sounded too close to "damn."

Thankfully, Richard quit fighting in high school and played football to work off his aggressions. He became a serious student and went on to graduate from a divinity college to become a Methodist minister enriching the spiritual lives of many people.

He like me is living proof that how people start out in life cannot predict how they finish.

After two years my career at Iron City School ended since Mama had other plans for my education. The formative years with poignant memories were my introduction to schooling. I had begun the process of growing the mind and making friends whom I would see again in the eighth grade as we all started high school.

CHAPTER 9

DONALSONVILLE ELEMENTARY

In September 1953 I began my five year attendance at Donalsonville Elementary School. Mama possibly sensed my affinity for the books and felt the larger institution could provide an improved learning opportunity. Soon I fit into my new school without missing a stride and started making life-long friends.

When Mama had made a decision, she would forcefully pursue a goal with little regard for obstacles. N.P. Malcom had been one of her teachers at Iron City School where she had reached about twenty-one years old when finishing high school. Her parents had held her out of school to work on the farm which resulted in the delayed graduation. Mr. Malcom surpassed her by only three-five years of age since teaching at Iron City School was his first job. Over the years he eventually advanced to Superintendent of Schools for the county.

Geographic boundaries separated the Iron City and Donalsonville school districts with our house residing about one mile from the boundary beyond which kids went to Donalsonville. She did not ask Mr. Malcom, but told him that I would attend Donalsonville Elementary for the coming year. He mentioned the boundary problem, and she committed to providing the wherewithal to transport me to it. Daddy purchased my first bicycle which I rode one mile each day to catch the school bus until the bike had worn out. Then my dependable two feet, Flatfoot and Flossie, who never broke down, became my transportation.

In the third grade, I started to connect with the books, and school became effortless with me having an abundance of A's and minimum B's on my report card. Getting along with teachers came natural, but I did not get close to any of them. Correspondingly, in high school no teacher really touched my button in a way that caused me to befriend them. Shyness and insecurities from the harsh realities of my past had given me a guarded personality, but the teachers seemed to always like the kid who usually kept his mouth shut and made way-above-average grades.

Mama, caring about my grades, always looked forward to seeing and signing my report cards, an involvement which inspired me to perform well and treasure her blessings. If Daddy learned about my grades, Mama would have told him since he never asked me about them nor commented on my work at school.

CHAPTER 10

HITTING FLIES/
CATCHING FLIES

W ho could have imagined the calamity that could be associated with innocently knocking fly balls in grammar school? The boys liked knocking flies, so roughly ten of us would come together during break times and participate. When a kid caught three fly balls, he had his turn at bat and knocked the softball to the others.

My turn at bat had arrived, and I began swatting away. After tossing the ball into the air, I swung, missed it, and struck a firm object: a seventh grader named Johnny Roberts. He, making an unwise choice of time and place, had walked behind me as I swung the bat. Apparently he could have had heavy thoughts on his brain, but in actuality he had a bat which hit him squarely in the upper part of his cranium. Thud! The contact, close to the fat end of the bat, maximized the impact causing disbelief on my part that his head did not fly spinning in the air toward the catchers.

What does a person do when struck viciously with a softball bat? He started running in circles with blood spurting from his wound.

What did I do? Standing there with my mouth open, I wondered whether the law sent kids to prison.

A teacher Mrs. Killian stood nearby, saw him in distress and grabbed his hand and arm to push him to the ground. It made no sense to allow the kid to keep getting blood all over the playground. She and the principal applied a compression bandage, loaded him up, and headed for Donalsonville Hospital where Doctor Jenkins, Baxley or Stewart had an emergency on the way.

He came back to school the next day, walking straight, wearing a bandage. What a relief! I did not need the baggage of crippling a fellow schoolmate, and he certainly would rather have a normal, straight-walking life.

The grade school version of harassment started with Johnny and his "gang" (names withheld to protect the complicit) trying to make my life miserable. They picked at me and made threats while displaying hateful facial expressions. Any rational person would have known Johnny's negligence caused the accident, but they had to act hostile for a while, an irritation which caused me to adopt a defensive posture of ignoring them.

The whack with the bat may have knocked sense into Johnny since during the coming years, he did well by becoming a minister and contributed to people's lives and their spiritual needs. My rationalization said the lick to the head had put the boy on the straight and narrow. Since high school our paths have not crossed, so Johnny has not thanked me for that tap on the head.

CHAPTER 11

HOG KILLIN'

Before food freezers farmers chose a cold day in the winter to replenish the meat supply; a time which the cold temperatures reduced bacteria activity and deterioration of the slaughter. The job required completion in one work day to further ensure retardation of spoilage. Circa 1950 with only an icebox to keep portions cool, the family either hung the meat in the smokehouse, cooked portions to a non-deterioration state, or consumed some in the next three-four days.

The quantity of work required a collective effort because a family working alone could not handle the work in the time allowed. Anderson and Janie Williams, Waver Love Trawick, Beulah Trawick Ward and other relatives whose names escape me pitched in to complete the task.

The kinfolks showed up as close to daybreak as possible to find Daddy by a roaring fire which he had started under a huge iron kettle that had been passed on by my Granddaddy Mills. It served as a water trough for the mule normally, but today the huge container would serve as a boiling pot to help remove the hair from the swine.

The day before, Daddy had penned the pig(s) separately and provided a last meal of each pig's choosing. A carefully placed shot between the eyes with a twenty-two rifle set the ball rolling. The men grabbed the beast, dragged him over to the boiling kettle and immersed him for ten to fifteen minutes.

Next, they carried the swine to the edge of the barn and hung the carcass on a rafter at the eves. The men scraped away the hair and cut the hog into portions meat lovers may recognize: hams, shoulders, bacon slabs, ribs, head, intestines, fat, pancreas, lungs, liver, heart and the head.

Then, they applied liquid Figaro meat cure to the hams, shoulders and bacon. The ribs, which the family would eat soon, Mama placed in the ice box. After curing, the men hung portions on sticks about the length and size of a broom handle and placed them on rafters six-seven feet off the ground in the smoke house. I did not learn why the building carried the term smokehouse since no one smoked meat there in my era. Perhaps the dirt floor made it practical for Granddaddy to smoke meat in his day.

By mid-morning the women built fires under two wash pots to cook the fat pieces to a crispy texture producing cracklings. They saved a portion of the yielded fat to make lye soap. Mama would serve cracklings at breakfast, or she would cook crackling bread. The lye soap "cake" had an orange, tan color with a texture that could file a saw. The term "a good scrubbing" could have originated from the use of lye soap. The soap came with two rules for washing: Do not scrub too vigorously nor too long, or else the outer layer of skin would disappear, and do avoid getting suds in the eyes, unless the bather had a need to walk about tapping with a cane.

The women cleaned a portion of the intestines by turning them wrong side out and washing them, plus scraping away the smelly feces, so the person grinding could use them as sausage casings. Each year Daddy borrowed Anderson Williams's sausage grinder which had become the community processor. They used shoulder meat and various parts of lean to stuff the sausage. Before grinding, the women added red pepper and other seasonings to the meat to create that fiery flavor which we always liked at morning breakfasts.

The grinder operator inserted meat into the feeder, grabbed a gathered sausage casing, slipped it over the exit pipe and turned the handle to grind the meat and push it into the casing. After the grinder operator completed the stuffing, the men draped the sausage links over sticks and hung them alongside the bacon and hams. The scrumptious sausage had a unique taste which no one can replicate today.

Near the end of the day, the women started processing the hog head by first removing the brains for fried brains and eggs at breakfast the next morning and then boiling the head. The bulk of the rest of the hog's head went into "hog head cheese," better known as souse. The women sorted the edible and inedible parts, mixed the edibles with seasonings, black pepper, red pepper and sage and stuffed the gob of goodies into a flour sack. For a week or longer the sack of meat, dripping and solidifying, hung in the smoke house; when Mama placed the sliced "loaf" on the table, we ate heartily.

Daddy always dug a hole in the back yard, away from the house, where they placed the contents of the intestines and inedible pieces of the swine. On a morning after a hog killin', Mama had dressed my brother Lloyd for a visit to the doctor, and he accidentally fell into one of those holes before it had been covered. What a mess! Mama had to clean and dress him again after she "attended" to him, an exercise which involved pain for the attendee.

Thus went the day of hog killin' with the family's and relatives' day's work producing wholesome food which we counted on to provide a portion of our meat needs for the coming months. Mama and Daddy returned the favors by helping the neighbors with their hog processing. Cooperation and dependence on others to complete a job bound folks together.

CHAPTER 12

CANE SYRUP

When people have long lives, they witness innovations coming and going. Sometimes if the new concepts have longevity, we only see them coming. We go before they go; e.g. television. Other times we see them go but are not around when they come; e.g., typewriters. When things have a short life, we see them come and go; e.g., eight track tapes. Syrup making, which farmers had done for generations, I saw go.

Breakfast time always found a pitcher of sugarcane syrup occupying the center of our table. In a homegrown tale, a teacher asked a young fellow in grammar school to describe a balanced meal for breakfast and he responded, "Syrup, biscuits and sow belly." To complement those foods, we also had grits and eggs on our breakfast table. Mama made our biscuits by hand, and Daddy sliced and buttered them. When we picked up one from the plate, the fresh homemade cow butter had already melted and was ready for sopping the cane syrup. When available, we used homemade sausage links for sopping, also.

When the sugarcane's sweetness peaked in the fall, folks used a knife and a stalk of cane for some delicious chewing. The chewer used the knife for cutting the outer bark from the stalk and to slice the stalk into "chewing joints." Since chewing cane with its sweet, unique juice was a mouthwatering treat, a three foot portion of a stalk disappeared fast.

With cane syrup having a rich history in the county, Mama talked of taking her lunch to school in a one gallon syrup bucket, a lunch box with a bale. The plentiful cans, a side benefit of the popularity of the cane syrup, had other uses: e.g., to carry fish bait, to store cooking ingredients in the kitchen, to carry corn to the chickens.

In the 1940s Daddy had taken on the duties of syrup maker for our cousin Anderson Williams who had a syrup-making operation. He tended the big vat cooker to ensure the syrup came out tasty with the right viscosity. Mr. Anderson lived only about a mile and a half away, proximity which gave me opportunities to watch syrup making. The syrup maker used a ladle, a vat full of cane juice, one-two feet deep and four-five feet square, and a similar vat beside it as the chief tools of syrup cooking. A wood fire provided the heat, and Anderson ground the cane with a grinder powered by a drive pulley and belt connected to a tractor.

Often farmers used a mule walking in a circle to power the grinder, a practice leftover from the previous years. In the latter 1960s, not far from Albany I remember passing a syrup operation with mule power. This animal power operation had to be among the last to survive.

We would dip jugs of cane juice out of the vat, store them in the fridge and drink the sweet liquid when cold. What a delicious drink! Downing a half gallon of the medium to dark green juice required no effort.

Mr. Anderson with his loud voice was a passionate, opinionated fellow who always wore a kind heart and overalls. His wife Janie was pure salt of the earth with cooking abilities that could turn common foods into delectable treats. There were no couples my folks liked to stop and visit more than them. Anderson's vociferous complaining about the pot holes in the highway from Rock Pond to Iron City including choice words for the county commissioners stands out well in my mind.

His camp house at Rock Pond was a community get-together site where every family brought a dish and Daddy, Sampson Waddell, Atwood Lane and Dixie Williams Jones provided down home picking, singing and entertainment. With God keeping the critters away and us out of danger, the kids played hide and seek in the woods.

Not having a store or access to major retail outlets, Mr. Anderson easily disposed of his stock of syrup each year among his legitimate local customers and at least some illegitimate ones. Moonshiners would arrive with trucks to purchase Anderson's remaining inventory since they could use it to replace sugar. Buying quantities of sugar through a retail store cast suspicion on those producing alcohol which made cane syrup usage a safer bet.

Around 1953 to 1955, Anderson stopped making syrup, and a memorable portion of life in Seminole County disappeared. Having to resort to "store bought" syrup, we went through scores of half gallon jugs of Blackburn Made Syrup produced by T.J. Blackburn, Jefferson, Texas. At breakfast I read the label on the jug so frequently that I will never forget it. Containing corn and cane syrup, it tasted acceptable, but it did not compare to the syrup which came from down the road. The company still thrives with its products carried by Amazon, Kroger and probably others who sell it along with a line of jellies, jams and similar items.

Over the years many families in the county had made syrup. Daddy once showed me a picture of his daddy helping my great Uncle Luke Spooner produce syrup. I suppose that was Pop's place and time to learn the trade.

Neighbors who cared for each other produced sugarcane syrup from the earth. The syrup buckets, the pitchers of syrup on the table, the cold sweet juice and the chewing of cane stalks are distant memories for those of us who experienced those treasured times. What a shame that we have to give up so much and pay so dearly for progress, but those costs are the irrevocable nature of life. God bless Mr. Anderson and his contribution to the well-being of the friends and neighbors who knew him.

CHAPTER 13

BISCUITS

A man once said that if the biscuits' contribution to his bulk disappeared, there would not be much left of him. Residents of Seminole County still view biscuits as a necessary dish in the food supply. Today cooks select premade, packaged biscuits from the frozen food lockers and take them home for a twenty-minute baking in the oven at three hundred seventy-five degrees, a practice which is causing the skill of making "catheads" (colloquial term) to disappear.

Until instant or ready-made came along, housewives routinely made a batch of biscuits in the morning. Effortlessly, Mama could roll and form a batch of biscuits in jig time. Watching her on so many occasions, I could not relate to the skill and know-how involved. Not long ago I tried to bake biscuits from scratch, and it became apparent that I could not simply decide to cook biscuits without first developing the expertise. Not having the proficiency, I could have used mine for door stops or muzzle loading a musket.

For generations mothers passed on the expertise of biscuit making to their daughters since preserving the skill was viewed as necessary to feed a family. I have no way of being sure, but I would wager Mama's biscuits tasted similar to my Grandmother Trawick's. Whatever differences existed could be charged to subtle changes in the ingredients.

Grandmother Mills, at a weight of no greater than a hundred pounds, had eleven children with two dying at birth. When they prepared biscuits in the morning, they cooked about twenty with a wooden stove. Grandma had four daughters who probably rotated biscuit-making duties as they grew up.

Grandmother had a biscuit board, a common household item of the day, carved out of one piece of a softwood. She used the board having dimensions of twelve inches wide by twenty-two inches long and a concave, oval shape to combine the ingredients and form biscuits. The size suggested that she and her daughters prepared large batches. The biscuit board lay on the floor of the old smoke house for years, but during my twenties, I saw it in the barn and had the idea of refurbishing it. To close a crack I used glue and then applied a pecan stain, a technique that produced a fine, old relic.

CHAPTER 14

MARTHA WHITE

Before television we enjoyed radio, the only source of electronic entertainment with mass appeal. In the 1950s our family gathered around the radio on Saturday and Sunday nights, times which had the best offerings. Art Linkletter's People Are Funny, The Arthur Godfrey (the Old Redhead) Show, Mr. Keen, Tracer of Lost Persons and The Grand Ole Opry were the family favorites.

Not listening to the radio to simply pass the time, the family eagerly anticipated and enjoyed a variety of programs. With radio we had to create a mental picture of the action transpiring based on what we heard. Mr. Keen came to life with the dialogue and a technician making sounds such as feet walking, doors closing and motors running. People were funny! Art had a natural talent of bringing out the natural humor in participants, and no one could have done the show but him. Arthur Godfrey with the distinctive laugh, a banjo and his affable style pulled in the listeners. The family declared The Grand Ole Opry as our favorite probably because of Daddy's intense love of country music which we absorbed as well.

When I remember the Opry, the Martha White jingle first comes to mind. "Now you'll bake right with Martha White. Goodness gracious good and light Martha White. You'll make better biscuits, cakes and pies with Martha White self-rising flour. The one all-purpose flour. Martha White self-rising flour has got Hot Rize." Hundreds of times the guest stars and host sang the commercial. Artists gathering around the microphone on stage and blasting away, usually including Roy Acuff, created the perception that advertisement could be a part of entertainment. The catchy jingle, "Duckhead work clothes wear like iron" became a part of the Opry format for an extended period, also.

The Opry performers enjoyed legend status including Red Foley, Little Jimmy Dickens, Webb Pierce, Faron Young, Jim Reeves, Ferlin Husky, Kitty Wells, Patsy Cline, Hawkshaw Hawkins and others who packed families around the "box" on Saturday nights. Minnie Pearl, Doctor Lou Childree and Rod Brasfield added comic relief. On one Saturday night near the beginning of his career, Elvis appeared but did not exactly woo the crowd.

In 1979 I had the privilege of taking Daddy and my brother Lloyd to the Opry, and they enjoyed it immensely. On the way home, Daddy commented that he could play a guitar and mandolin just as well as any of them. Agreeing, I said that it would be difficult to distinguish any differences between his playing and theirs. Pop played his instruments well.

Wayne Raney and Lonnie Glosson, both songwriters and singers, had a syndicated radio program where they played their harmonicas and sang. Both had long careers in country entertainment. Lonnie Glosson made appearances on Hee Haw in his last years after achieving fame through the huge number of mail order harmonicas they had sold. Jerome listened to them promoting guitars and sent fifteen dollars for one, a purchase which made him the only sibling who tried to claim musical talent. Unfortunately, Daddy did not pass his gift down through his genes. Jerome learned to strum it and tried to sing but only for home audience consumption.

Having the old Truetone radio provided a major barrier between us and boredom. Jerome lay on the floor listening circa 1955 when he called me over to hear a song, Elvis's "Heartbreak Hotel." Hearing the song, I liked his music and could sense his potential having a totally new sound unlike any we had ever heard.

Soon the ducktail hair styles mimicking Elvis showed up and influenced local Willie Hunt to do the "do." The rest of the teenagers had to warm up to it carefully since they had to deal with the opinions of mama and daddy.

The three times Elvis performed on the Ed Sullivan Show had a huge impact on the music and entertainment industries. Mama and Daddy seemed to like the performance with reservations while the rest of us, having never witnessed youth going crazy over a performer, loved the show. What a performance! The planet did not go to hell as prognosticators tried to have society think; the going-to-hell thing became a product of today's domain.

In 1957 Daddy purchased a Philco television from Peg Drake who had a store on Hwy 39 by the railroad tracks. Paying a hefty $375 for the television, antenna rotor and outside antenna, Daddy committed big bucks from our family's budget. Residents could buy a new car for under $2,000, so TV's were comparatively expensive. We became the second house in the neighborhood to own a set with Raymond and Nettie Doris Spooner Simmons buying the first one. When we went to their house to watch wrestling, Daddy, Mama and I were immediately hooked. Watching Gorgeous George tossing around the other wrestlers had great appeal, but our naiveté did not suspect the fake nature of the matches. Wanting to climb into the ring with them, Mama became disturbed when the villain wrestler seemingly abused the good guy.

Daddy's priority of purchasing a television and having no bathroom made our house the only one in the community, and possibly the county, so furnished. Looking back, I have to ask, "What criteria did he use to make that decision?"

Daddy chose between a television and a bathroom, whereas today televisions are often found in bathrooms. As the old Virginia Slims television commercial used to say, "You've come a long way, baby."

The television brought the family a new entertainment medium. No longer having to visualize the radio programs, we could see the action. Saturday afternoons I watched Dizzy Dean and Pee Wee Reese calling a Yankees game. My life had changed. I would rather stay at home and watch baseball than go to town with Mama and Daddy.

These legends were among the best sports broadcasters who ever sat behind a microphone. With Pee Wee as the straight man and Dizzy's tales of growing up on the farm and playing ball, they mesmerized the audience. Dizzy, a retired pro pitcher, seemingly had done and seen it all.

Mickey Mantle, Roger Maris, Hank Bauer, Bobby Richardson, Yogi Berra, Elston Howard, Moose Skowron, Clete Boyer, Tony Kubek with Casey Stengal coaching comprised the best team that played baseball in the era. Each day when the Dothan Eagle came, I checked the players' statistics and could practically recite them from memory. They played before money, drugs and egos began damaging the game.

Bobby Richardson who seldom knocked a home run cleared the fence by inches in a World Series game, a feat that caused the crowd to go wild and brought the team to victory.

My favorite player Mickey Mantle had the reputation of being the fastest to first base. With the audience aware he could knock one out of the park at any time, each trip to the batter's box brought wild anticipation from his fans. Then along came a younger Roger Maris who challenged him on the home run statistics.

On Saturday mornings I watched Fury with its intro: "The story of a horse and a boy who loved him" with a young Peter Graves (later star of television's "Mission Impossible"). On Saturday nights

"Gunsmoke" dominated, depicting Matt taking care of the bad guys supported by Chester, Doc and Miss Kitty. The whole country loved the show, so our family could always be found in front of the television at ten o'clock on Saturday nights to watch the "oater" which lasted in excess of twenty years. Richard Boone played one bad dude as Paladin with his gun for hire, ironically with a heart and integrity. On Monday nights "I Love Lucy" owned the audiences with riotous humor that the four stars created effortlessly. The best comedy show ever, by all accounts, draws a large audience today with reruns.

Circa 1959 color television debuted which mattered not to us since the color televisions cost dearly. Besides, Matt and Paladin did their best work in black and white. The NBC peacock, known as the network's symbol for color, I saw in full spectrum regalia only after leaving the farm.

Daddy had extra money from top soil that he sold to the construction company that was paving the road by our house and purchased our first new Ford Truck and our first food freezer in 1954

A ringer washer, a gas stove and two gas heaters eventually made their way into the house. Upward mobility had struck at our domicile, and we did not comprehend it.

The new-fangled appliances came with surprises. Once, Mama caught her arm in the washing machine ringer and had to remove it to drive to the doctor alone, but the accident only gave it a thorough mashing. The ringer washing machines must have helped originate the expression, "got her tits in a ringer."

With the added appliances, occasionally a repair man had to be utilized. Minter Radio Shop fixed the radio when a tube blew. James Alligood, our mail carrier, repaired the television about every six months when one of its tubes expired. Hubert Grant repaired the electric well when it quit running. L. T. Hudson, an electrician, came to the house only once or twice for a minor reason that escapes my memory; we had few electrical circuits to repair.

With great risk, Daddy would occasionally substitute a penny in our fuse box until he could purchase a new fuse. With this unsafe practice, the good Lord stood guard and prevented the house from burning.

When our electrical appliances consisted of a light bulb hanging in the middle of every room with a long string to switch it on and off, a radio, an electric iron, and the water pump, I recall seeing an electric bill of four dollars. Adding the above luxuries, it soared above six dollars, the cost of progress.

When I became taller and could reach the string to switch the lights off and on, I had a benchmark for measuring my growth.

The radio, television and other electric wonders changed the world and people's lives. I feel fortunate to have lived in the era and to have witnessed the advent of new electronic wizardry. We senior citizens have had the blessings to witness a long list of innovations from a light bulb hanging in the middle of a room to GPS which can track our every movement.

CHAPTER 15

EMMETT WARD

An unforgettable fellow of my childhood was an Iron City merchant Emmett Ward whose business our family frequented in the '50s. Visiting the establishment in the '30s, a first cousin recalled Mr. Emmett's business being there, but I have no knowledge of the store's origin.

Mr. Ward could be described physically as a small man, possessing a dowager's hump, perennially wearing suspenders, and bald with only wisps of hair still waving in the breeze. On Sundays about the only time anyone saw Mr. Emmett out of the store, he would wear a suit and a bowler hat for church. Being a devout Christian, he picked up children around town, transported them to Sunday school and gave them change for the offering if they had none.

Visiting the store in the '50s, our family purchased the basics of the time such as gas, kerosene, sugar, flour, baking powder, bleach, salt, tea and spices. He offered cold drinks immersed in ice at the front of the store in a chest type, lift top Coca Cola cooler. Royal Crowns, Nehi grape, Nehi orange and Coke dominated the soft drink market with ice cold drinks tasting oh so refreshing in the summer.

Items including canned goods, wash tubs, thread, baking soda, chewing gum, cheese and cracker jacks made up the bulk of the balance of inventory. With only 1,000 to 1,500 square feet of operating space, customers could shop the store in little time.

Revealing the building's previous use, a metal baseplate on the floor at the entrance door displayed the name of a bank which occupied the building before Mr. Ward did. The town, a thriving municipality back in the late 19th and early 20th centuries, originally had the name of Brooklyn which the residents changed to Iron City about 1900. The name probably originated from a quantity of iron ore found during an excavation.

To be sure of the correct total to charge, Emmett would pump the gas. Turning a crank on the side of the pump to clear the register and start the motor, he activated the machine. Having a firm grip on his money, he always pumped the patron's gas with no "pumping and telling him" allowed. The expression, "he was so tight he squeaked when he walked," fit him well.

Donalsonville merchants sold merchandise cheaper, but Emmett would give Daddy credit. He needed a credit account, so our family could slide through the part of the year which had low or non-existent cash flow. Writing the credit charges down on a slip, Mr. Emmett was trusted by his customers to keep the tally. When the account holders paid, they received the pieces of paper.

With his having a fireplace in the back of the building, customers would often find him snuggled by the warmth when they entered in the winter time. A distinct homey feeling permeated the store with a coal-fired iron stove and fireplace adding to the ambience. A well-worn coal bucket he kept in the area for replenishing the fires with the coal pile outside a near door. Striking a Norman Rockwell pose, he hunkered by the stove or fireplace with his cup of warm milk or a concoction of the same with a raw egg, common among elders of the time.

My family visiting Emmett Ward's store attracted me to John Goodwin's ice cream shop which occupied the space next door. While

Daddy and Mama bought essentials, I would ask them for ice cream change for a trip to Mr. Goodwin's. A one scoop chocolate cone cost a nickel, two scoops, a dime; the variety of three flavors offered included chocolate, vanilla and strawberry.

Being the only place I could buy ice cream at the age of five-eight years old, I attempted to ride with anyone who went to Emmett's for groceries, sometimes hiding on the back floorboard of the car until my ruse was discovered.

On a lucky day, a train passed through town while I licked my cone sitting on the edge of a circular, masonry water trough left over from the horse and buggy days.

Emmett Ward, an honest, hardworking businessman and community leader, who was held in esteem by the townsfolk, complemented Iron City of the '50s. His name, as a school board member, appears on Mama's diploma from Iron City High School in 1929. In the late '60s or first half of the '70s, Mr. Emmett closed the store and turned the page on another chapter in Iron City history.

CHAPTER 16
SCREWWORMS

Screwworms, possessing a capacity to enter an animal through an open wound or its nostrils, received their name from the screw-like shape of their bodies. The screwworm fly and its larvae menaced the animals and the farmers' livelihoods in the 1950s and earlier.

Entering swine through wounds where the flies would lay eggs, the larvae practiced their flesh-destroying habits. Screwworm larvae had voracious appetites for living tissue, eventually killing the animals and creating a substantial financial loss for the farmers. Watching a pig walk around with the worms eating away at it, created an unpleasant sight and a sense of helplessness because farmers had no effective remedy.

The castration of male pigs, a risky activity, exposed raw flesh to the introduction of eggs from the screwworm fly. Daddy would pour a blue liquid called Smearex on the wound which would offer protection, but the pigs often would head to a mud wallow which washed it away, an activity that diminished the benefits.

The family had a smoke house, a food bank, in which we hung hams and bacon sides for future consumption. Brushing on liquid

Figaro cured the meat and made it unlikely to deteriorate with its taste producing an unpleasant dish for flies. In spite of this application, skipper maggots, first cousins to the screwworm flies, would infest the ham or bacon at times. As Mama found the parasites eating away when she cut a piece of bacon, she would excise that portion, and we would eat the rest. The family minimized waste and consumed all edible food since it was so precious in those days.

Mama told a story of a woman who contracted a screwworm egg in her nose that multiplied and ate her brain. With this nuisance being around, such an incident could have easily occurred. The pest still infests areas of South America where humans infrequently die from screwworm infestations.

In the mid to latter '50s, the Department of Agriculture developed a remedy for ridding our country of screwworms. Planes released boxes of sterile male flies that would mate with the females, an act which resulted in no offspring and eventually led to their extinction. Finding one of the boxes in our field, confirmed to me that help was on the way.

CHAPTER 17

CHICKEN HAWKS

The name chicken hawk fit them well; they killed and ate chickens, thievery which forced farm families to battle these wily predators that wanted to share our food supply. Normally they would feed on other foul and animals, but when hungry, they regarded poultry as just another source of nourishment.

Circa 1950 we had a chicken pen which was about fifty feet wide and seventy-five feet long that included a chicken house with suspended boards for roosting. Located in one corner of the house were wooden boxes on the ground where the chickens would lay their eggs and hatch their young. Standing about six feet tall, a fence constructed of chicken wire kept the poultry in and a majority of critters out.

Unknowingly at the time, we raised the original "range chickens" for which today's stores charge a premium. Not caged and fed only corn, they had abundant exercise and tasted better than today's caged and sometimes steroid-laced birds.

One rooster handled the propagation duties because a second rooster would have produced a competition in which one would eventually kill the other. A busy bird, with little sleep the cock serviced fifty to seventy-five chickens. Being a typical male, he would "tune them out" when the hens asked questions or voiced complaints he did not want to hear.

Swooping down from above, the hawks coveted the younger, smaller pullets. Their size made them desirable because the hawks could carry them away easier and faster. These predators, with a risk of exploding in a hail of birdshot always present, knew that time was not on their side when invading the domain of a farm family.

As fried chicken for dinner and scrambled eggs for breakfast to complement the grits, biscuits, sausage and syrup, the chickens held a position of importance in diets and some financial transactions. Poultry and eggs were a medium of exchange which housewives swapped for flour, sugar and other basics when the rolling store came. (The rolling store of the day was a retail business on wheels offering basic items such as sugar, salt, flour and baking soda.)

Hearing the chicken hawk's piercing, elevated screams caused immediate consternation for the family and the chickens. Alerted by the noise, every chicken in the pen would squat as flat to the ground as possible, a reaction to their sensing the hawk had come close. Daddy would either yell for one of my older brothers to retrieve the shotgun, or he would run for it to prevent the hawk from stealing a chicken. He referred to the hawks as striking the chickens, meaning sinking their claws into one, eating it on the spot or flying away for a feast on a nearby tree limb dependent on the bird's size.

Mr. Hawk, cognizant of the risk of diving into the chicken yard, appeared on days when his appetite had gotten the best of him. If a family member retrieved the shotgun fast enough, chicken hawk feathers floated in the air and a limp carcass lay on the ground. The dead bird provided a feast for the cats and thereby supported recycling.

The chicken house played another important role in preserving the family's health and well-being. When I contracted the chicken pox, Mama led me to the chicken house in the early evening and instructed me to squat under the front side of the roost. With her making a noise on the back side of the roost, the chickens flew over me. As Mama predicted, the chicken pox disappeared in a period of days, which the doubtful may view as foolishness. Perhaps excellent timing delivered a miracle cure? My grandmother had used the same practice with Mama.

Chicken hawks, chickens and chicken pox added to the charm of farm life in the mid- twentieth century. Such a far away and different existence as compared to the present, that life was a simple world which farm folks, who lived it, recall fondly.

CHAPTER 18

NANERS AND CRACKERS

About 1953 Mama; Mrs. Vada Spooner; her daughters Nan, nine years old; Susan, seven and I, eight years old loaded into the car and headed to Jacksonville, Florida. Occupying the front were Mama and Mrs. Vada while we children did what children do in the back seat. With Mama having several relatives to visit in Jacksonville including two sisters, two brothers, an uncle and their families, which were also related to Mrs. Vada, with excitement and anticipation our group motored toward the big city.

An afternoon found us at Uncle Ed's house with Mama and Mrs. Vada visiting him and his wife in the living room. Receiving bananas as a treat, we kids walked out the front door and toward the road to eat them away from the adults. As we strolled out toward the street, Susie and I gulped down our "naners;" whereas, Nan preferred to nibble and had eaten only a bite of her snack.

Out of nowhere came one of those unscripted happenings which entangles lives. A car coming down the road in the lane next to the house motivated Nan to have an attack of impulsiveness as it came closer. With an amazing feat of timing, she threw her naner at the car, a toss which caught the right edge of the windshield and left a stringing splatter across it. The perfect throw had obstructed a major portion of the windshield and caused the driver to pop the brakes.

With three emotions flashing their way through our brains, we digested the wanton act: first, the hands across the mouth with "aaw-wwwooo," next, the laughter behind the hands and when the car stopped, pants-wetting fear.

Noticing the car stopping and beginning to back up, all three of us thought we should be any place but there. The "Bogeyman," figuratively speaking, was about to come for us and do evil things.

Making the straightest route possible to the front door, I referenced my brain's library of previous such encounters that instructed me to head for refuge in proximity to Mama's dress tail. Coming through the front door, running wide open, I headed for safety under a bed to hedge my bet.

No sooner had I settled down in my seclusion than Mama stood by the bed saying, "Come out from under there. What's wrong?" Bouncing out, realizing that Mama asking the second time had to be avoided, I stood at attention and prepared to deliver my best explanation. This commotion being a rare time of my innocence, I chose spilling the beans as the best alternative. "Nan did it. She threw a naner at a car, and they are coming in to get us," I exclaimed.

Walking back into the living room, we saw Uncle Ed looking out the front window. Sitting at the end of the driveway for a minute, pondering what had happened, the occupants chose to drive away. What a relief!

Uncle Ed offered an explanation, "They probably saw the Georgia tag and said, "More of those crazy "Crackers"" and figured it was not worth the trouble."

Taking notice that Nan and Susan had disappeared, Mrs. Vada headed out the back door to conduct a search which included Uncle Ed's chicken house. (The substantial land area encompassed by Jacksonville permitted chicken houses in sections of the city limits per zoning regulations.) Mrs. Vada found them squatting among the chickens with Nan having a sheepish look as if she had laid an egg. Well, she had. After they came out, we all had a robust belly laugh.

What an adventure! A young girl's sudden decision to toss her naner had created a commotion, and a family of Crackers from Seminole County had enjoyed an exciting day in Jacksonville.

Having visited with Susan at her mother's visitation not long ago, she mentioned the incident, and we both fondly relived the day. Kids sometimes find amusement in the strangest of ways, places and times, and their brains lock away the outrageous happenings.

CHAPTER 19

THE SANDBAR

Our favorite swimming hole which sometimes was referred to as the Miller Sandbar, families simply called the Sandbar, a cool body of creek water that attracted the youth and adults. The excitement of a trip there put smiles on faces in anticipation of the raucous fun and the cooling water. While fighting the gnats, the older folks visited while chiefly the young enjoyed the inviting creek.

To access the diving board, swimmers had to squeeze between two trunks of a split cypress tree. They would jump from the board and land in cool, clear spring water which originated from the springs that fed the waterway giving it the name of Spring Creek.

A rope hung from the cypress tree that secured the diving board. For accessing the rope, a swimmer would have to step over to the tree, grab it and pull it back to the bank. A brief run along the bank would propel the swimmer out across the water where he would jump with a five or six foot drop and a splash. Flying across the water in the air brought exhilaration as the swimmer dived into the creek. Those first timers who could not muster the courage to release the rope confronted a serious molestation by the cypress tree as the rope returned to its normal hanging location.

Only thirty to forty yards south of the diving board, a crowd congregated at a sandy bottom, three-five feet deep spot, which attracted swimmers who wanted to splash and languish in the water. On overflow days when the splashers appeared to be wall to wall, the act of moving through the area paralleled charging through a football line.

Living a mile away, Joe Dick swam often, if not daily, ultimately developing the skills of a Johnny Weismuller. Slow fish could not match Joe's speed, and his graceful dives created "not much splash" as the Olympic judges often said on TV. I avoided the frustration of trying to swim and dive as well as him.

Just upstream of the diving board, where my brothers, relatives and friends congregated, lay an oak tree that had long ago fallen across the creek. With the tree trunk exposed above the water to allow the group to sit on it and slip into the creek when desired, it became their hanging out place.

For fun the swimmers tossed objects such as Coca Cola bottles into the eight-ten feet deep water and retrieved them. A deposit on the bottom contained clay that these teenagers liked to bring back up and throw at each other in mud fights.

As they decided to take on the challenge of swimming, many children learned to swim at the Sandbar including me. Having mastered the classic dog paddle as my starting point, eventually, I opted to learn to swim as the big boys. Without lessons I applied grit and determination and soon swam similarly to others except Joe Dick. Realizing my shortage of his level of expertise, I managed to maneuver well among the other swimmers.

On Saturdays and Sundays, lunch groups delighted in the food and fellowship of the times. Under the trees, picnickers set up tables and dropped tail gates to support a spread of gourmet country eating. Fried chicken, black-eyed peas, snap beans, hoecake cornbread, new potatoes, sliced tomatoes, okra, turnip greens and ambrosia never tasted as scrumptious as they did there. The swimming built a fierce appetite, and we had the best cooks in the county. When supply met demand, everyone crammed their stomachs with the delicious food. The desserts such as: pecan pie, pound cake, egg custard, coconut pie, coconut cake, blackberry pie, chocolate divinity fudge with pecans on top and chocolate cake topped off the feast.

During these days, we shared some of the finest, most memorable times of our young lives, not realizing it as we lived them. When I drove back fifteen-twenty years ago, the owners had blocked the access road to the sandbar, a barrier that had closed this rural institution. Interest in swimming there had waned over the years, so the closing caused no significant regrets for anyone. The memories lived, but the inimitable times at the Sandbar had slipped away forever.

CHAPTER 20

THAT "COTTON PICKIN'" COTTON

At 5:30 a.m. Daddy saying, "Get up," interrupted the dream of the moment. He only had to say it once, and I hit the floor to throw on my clothes. Too often I had witnessed him having to come back and wake my brothers over and over, so I had resolved to not put him and me through that senseless game.

Both brothers had passed eighteen and had other jobs, therefore, Daddy had unceremoniously given me the job of right hand man at the age of eleven which I took seriously. Mama often said, "Money does not grow on trees." Today, the dollars were in the cotton patch on stalks, and we had to harvest them.

Having finished dressing in a jiffy, I headed for the breakfast table. With Daddy doing his job of buttering biscuits, and Mama moving bacon, eggs and grits to the table, we sat down to some grub. The meal was the same o' same o', but the food tasted delicious, and it would provide the energy to keep our motors running until lunch.

Since between-meal snacks had not been introduced to our farm life, we could not count on them for a boost.

With Daddy's knuckles pressed against his forehead, he muttered a largely unintelligible, ten second blessing which I never fully translated. The ending of "For Christ's sake, Amen" was as far as my careful listening could discern. If the family moved slowly and he had something pressing to do, he said the blessing, ate and headed out the door before the rest of us sat down.

Daddy finished breakfast usually before Mama and me, headed out the door to crank the '54 Ford pickup truck and was on the way to pick up the "hands" with a portion living in Iron City and the rest residing nearby. He always picked up my buddy and first cousin Jimmy Williams who picked cotton to earn spending money.

While he was gone, I fed the pigs and milked the cow. It did not take but roughly ten minutes to pump a gallon of milk out of old Butterfly, our Guernsey cow. Standing there patiently, she knew her job and I knew mine.

About 6:30 or 7:00 a.m., we grabbed a cotton drag sack and a cotton sheet as we headed to the cotton patch. Today, natives would call it a field but in my day most everyone clung to the old term patch.

South Georgia mornings commonly had heavy dews which caused the pickers to encounter a wetting from the moisture on the cotton stalks. When a row went through bottom land where the stalks were taller and contained more moisture, we received a dunking. Within twenty minutes the clothes on our bodies were dripping from sweat mixed with dew. This wetting of us required until about ten o'clock for the sun to dry as we worked.

The skilled hands would "carry" two rows of cotton which meant that they picked two rows at a time, crawling or standing between them. Alternating standing and crawling on our knees, Jimmy and I always chose one row. When the back became tired, the knees came to the rescue. As the ground reached peak heat in the afternoon, the knees would feel as if they were burning which prompted standing on our feet and occasionally stopping briefly in the shade of a tall cotton stalk to cool them.

For the remuneration of three cents per pound of cotton, we worked eleven-twelve hours in the sunshine and endured ninety to one hundred degree heat. A top hand could pick two hundred pounds in a day with a few pickers exceeding it. Jimmy and I picked about one hundred ten to one hundred thirty pounds. Jimmy's arms, an inch or two longer than mine, gave him the capability of picking a greater amount than I could or that was my justification.

Willie C. King was the same age as Jimmy and I were, so we would choose rows adjacent, shoot the breeze about whatever and sing when we were inclined. As we picked the same old cotton out of the same old cotton burrs over and over, boredom entered our young minds. Pick the cotton and drag the sack, which had a strap that went across the shoulder, was the routine. When the sack became full, we emptied it on reaching the end of the row where the sheets were placed to save carrying the load across the field on our shoulders.

My pit bull Chief always had a presence in the patch, and infrequently he would roust a rabbit and a chase ensued. Daddy did not want him running rabbits in the cotton patch because he would knock cotton from the stalks and onto the ground which created a financial loss, so Chief received abundant scoldings.

Come noon time our stomachs announced loudly "Time for dinner," not lunch, a term I learned later in life. Daddy would take the hands to Barber's store on Highway 39. They would load up on Vienna sausage, sardines, saltines, pork & beans, cold drinks, honey buns and cinnamon rolls, not a well-balanced diet, but one that was affordable and available. Some workers brought a lunch bucket from home.

Daddy would bring everyone back to our house to have their lunches under the china berry trees where they would eat, talk and try to steal a quick nap before Daddy headed back to the "blazing furnace" with the rest of us following.

Daddy, Mama, Jimmy and I ate together. A typical meal would have been creamed corn, ham or chicken, butter beans or peas cooked with stewed okra, hoe cake corn bread, sliced tomatoes and pound cake or egg custards for dessert. With Mama's delicious food and sweet tea filling the table, we munched down with gusto. Five hours in the cotton patch had produced an appetite that could be pushed around in a cart.

After eating, Jimmy and I would stretch out on the linoleum floor to close our eyes. Our dirty clothes prevented reclining on the furniture, so the floor was the only choice.

About 1:00 p.m. Daddy said, "Let's go," and we all began moving.

During the long, hot afternoons, the hands would raid a nearby persimmon tree for leaves to put in their hats, so I took heed and followed suit. If our heads were cooler, the whole body felt more comfortable. The persimmon leaves provided moisture which had a cooling effect when it evaporated.

Come 6:30 or 7:00 p.m., we stopped picking and weighed the cotton. To secure it for weighing, the hands would help each other gather the cotton in the sheets and tie opposing diagonal corners of the sheet. The weighing mechanism consisted of a six feet long lead pipe with a counterbalance scale attached in the middle. Using the pipe with the scales and hook attached in the center, two workers would lift the sheet of cotton from the ground. Daddy positioned a hundred pound "pea" on the scale to determine the cotton's weight. The pea's weight, being only a pound or two, had the effect of one hundred pounds when placed on the scales. Daddy kept moving the pea along the scales until he achieved a balance point. When the scales balanced or leveled, he would read the weight, and I would write it down in a book by the name of the hand. If the weight of the cotton exceeded two hundred pounds, a second one hundred pound pea was added to the scale.

On Fridays Daddy traveled to the bank to obtain cash bills and change for paying the hands. After the day's weighing, he sat at our dining table and calculated the pickers' pay for the week. Then, he went outside and paid each worker twenty-five to thirty-five dollars for a full week's work. Daddy tried to avoid cheating anyone, so he often told the workers that he would rather give them a penny than take one away. If a mistake were claimed, he investigated and made things right immediately.

With me receiving the same price per pound that he paid the hands, the seemingly huge sum of perhaps fifteen-twenty dollars in my hands was truly rewarding because I had earned it.

When the mechanical cotton pickers entered the market place circa 1958 and they had been proven, Daddy hired a contractor to pick our cotton. The first time a machine arrived at our farm, I excitedly ran out and gave it a big, sloppy kiss, a gesture which expressed true love at first sight. An era had passed, so the sweat and back-breaking work would now exist in the yesteryear as a tainted memory.

Elements of that way of life needed to pass because I never felt good regarding the impoverished hands and their positions in life. We lived in poverty, but not as deeply as they. Our country's ingenuity and prosperity have elevated us all to a better standard of living – thanks to the Grace of God.

What is missing today, especially for the young, is available opportunities to struggle and do the challenging work. Struggle builds integrity and values that make a person stronger and appreciative of the benefits of success. I still value, revere and take care of the material possessions we own because I know from where those things and our status in life came.

CHAPTER 21

HOEING PEANUTS

Before herbicides, there were two ways to control unwanted vegetation in the peanut patch: plowing and hoeing. Plowing removed ninety-five percent of the weeds and grass, but the rest we hoed or removed by hand. Setting his plows about the width of a penny matchbox apart, Daddy plowed the young weeds and grass recognizing that with one bobble he plowed up peanut plants, and we lost money. In spite of the close plowing, manual removal was necessary because vegetation still found a way to grow between plants. Labor intensive with us having long hours, dirty, sweaty clothes and a sense of never finishing, hoeing grass challenged the body and the spirit.

The plants to be removed from our crops included coffee weeds, tea weeds, pusley, sandspurs, cockleburs, trellis and the hated crab grass. Our neighbors had bull grass and Johnson grass which Daddy had tried intensely to keep out of our patches because those grasses were especially hardy. In spite of our diligent efforts, they started creeping into our crops in my late teen years via their seeds being included in the commercial seeds that we used to plant the crops.

The hoe was used for removing grass that could be accessed without chopping peanut plants. The corner of the hoe we applied skillfully to remove vegetation from between peanut plants. Daddy taught us that we must remove the root, or the plant would just sprout out again. If we could not hack out the root with the hoe, we leaned over and pulled the plant up with our hands. Crabgrass, which could not be hoed, we extracted with the aid of the index finger, the middle finger and the thumb. We plunged two fingers into the ground on either side of the root, and our thumbs helped pull it out. When I went to the opera, a "horse opera," my rough- hewn manicure would never impress. If a rainy period were in process, we would lay the crab grass on top of the peanut plants to ensure that the roots could not access the ground and start growing again.

At the end of the rows of peanuts, Daddy would roll one of his Prince Albert's and puff on it for a minute. (Smoking was the reason he died of lung cancer at eighty-two. There was only one healthy use of Prince Albert, scraping the peanut plows with the can).

I would lean on my hoe, and have a drink of water from the jug setting at the end of the rows. An hour or two after arriving in the patch, the water was no longer ice cold because it gravitated to the temperature of the air around us.

Sometimes taking a watermelon to the patch in the afternoon, we experienced a taste beyond delicious because of our high levels of hunger and thirst.

My brother Jerome left Daddy and me to do the hoeing alone when he turned eighteen and I was eleven. Not missing the trellis plants he would bury in the row where I walked, I missed his help since the peanut fields seemingly got larger. When I stepped on one of Jerome's dirt-covered trellis plants, it gave a real zinger with its stickers to my bare feet which brought a commitment for revenge on my part. Whereas, I began turning the wheels in my brain to get revenge and have my laugh; and I did.

When the grass had gained an advantage, Daddy occasionally hired help with the hoeing. A first cousin Jimmy Williams joined us every summer to earn spending money at three dollars per day. His presence made the days shorter as we would talk and dream beyond the peanut patch. We counted on our present status to not be "That's all there is." Fortunately our leisure times together diminished the sweat and misery of hoeing penders. (Penders is an old colonial term for peanuts which was often used in my day).

Putting the peanuts into the Tom's toasted peanut package was a multi-step process that I had the "pleasure" of being a part of in the '50s and '60s. In late summer after the nuts reached maturity, we harvested the crop with a peanut combine and sold them to a peanut processor who shelled them and resold the product to food processors. Today I like to joke with friends that I had my first encounter with a "hoe," which was not the orgasmic kind, when I was only six years old. A fond recollection but certainly not one I would ever want to relive.

CHAPTER 22
CUT THE MULE

Cut the Mule was the name of the game at Hill Pace's service station in Iron City where farmers gathered every Sunday morning. A mundane diversion, by today's standards, brought folks together to socialize. The gentlemen included Lewis Roberts, Harry Ard, Ed Ard, Marsden Strickland, Sampson Waddell, Les Kid, Alva Cordell, Foy Rabun and Daddy. Hanging around, I listened to the conversations, watched cars go by and explored the garage in the back of the building.

The conversations ranged from the correct depth to plant corn, to the best way to treat screwworms, to tales of their favorite dog, to complaining about the price of medicine with not a note of disharmony. These guys, who rearranged the truth at times, liked each other's company and the camaraderie, but out of deference no one challenged the veracity.

Starting with numbers in a hat representing the number of players, in succession the gentlemen would draw the numbers. The numbers, one through the number of participants, a player wrote in a column. Each player in turn had an opportunity to "cut" a number from the list with the person cut last assigned to draw first. Pulling a six ounce Coke from the ice box comprised the drawing.

With Coca Cola bottling plants spread across the country, each facility's bottles had the name of the city and state where produced on the bottom. Buying a Coke in St. Louis and trading it for the one cent deposit in a distant town occurred with normal travel. The resident bottler used whatever empty "deposit" bottles came in to fill and sell additional Cokes along with the ones which had been produced with the local town name on the bottom. The practice populated cold drink boxes across the country with bottles of varied origins.

With each player betting a quarter, the man who drew the bottle with the farthest city on the bottom won the pot. By listening to them reading the cities and states on the bottom of the bottles, I received U.S. geography lessons. Not necessarily buying the Cokes, the players could just return them to the box unopened after registering the destination with the other guys. Apparently the game began well before my day and had been played for decades.

An exceptionally busy working man in a community where everyone worked hard, Mr. Hill stood out from the crowd. For him as others, dedicated labor was the tariff they paid to feed and care for their families. From their house about a hundred yards down the street, his wife Beulah would bring him lunch every day. Mr. Hill pumped gas, cleaned windshields, checked oil and performed vehicle maintenance for customers.

His oil change rack located outside the back of the garage required him to listen carefully for a customer to drive up to a gas pump. Gas customers interrupted the oil changes with Mr. Hill pumping the gas and returning when finished. Loving to fish, he would be gone for an afternoon occasionally which left Beulah to run the station, and oil changes waited until the next day.

The game "cut the mule" at Hill Pace's service station was a bona fide Iron City institution. Devoted, down-to-earth farmers accumulated placing their pressing problems on the shelf while enjoying fellowship and playing a simple game which helped bind them together.

CHAPTER 23

DEATH OF A FRIEND

I n a rural community still lacking phone service in a significant percentage of houses, bad news of losing our seventh grade class member could travel fast. Other than a kid and family moving from the area, this was the first time we students had seen a classmate leave on Friday and not ever come back. His loss took a toll on us. Breaking the calm in this South Georgia County, the horrible misfortune happened on a Sunday afternoon in 1958.

Walking one mile back from Barber's country store where they had purchased a gift for their mother's birthday, the Lewis brothers, Robert, Malcolm and Leroy, looked forward to delivering the surprise. Walking three abreast near the right side of the road but in the traffic right of way, they tempted fate. Robert walked closer to the center of the road, with Leroy and Malcom, near the edge.

As luck would have it that day, along came a car driven by Bill Roberts, known to take a drink of liquor. While I waited in the truck, Daddy had shared a tipple or two with him at the Log Cabin near Iron City when they happened to cross paths. Bill had possibly downed alcohol that tragic day.

The truth dying with those involved, no one today understands what exactly happened. Perhaps Bill in the dark, accompanied by his wife and daughter, did not see them until too late to jerk the wheel. The boys could have been talking loud and were unaware of the sound of the engine and tires approaching.

The impact sent Robert's body up on the hood of the car, traumatically broke Leroy's leg at the knee and injured Malcom's elbow. At the last second, one anecdote suggested, Robert tried to push the brothers out of the path, the heroism sounding like an act the Robert we loved would attempt.

Walking two blocks from Donalsonville Elementary School to Evans Funeral home, our seventh grade class attended the service. The friend we played with last Friday now lay silent and unmoving in the casket generating unreal sensations in my young brain. Robert should be playing softball and kickball and participating in all the things we did at school, but abruptly those times could now only exist in our memories.

The family, Raymond, Malcolm, Leroy, Jake and his wife, being taken terribly with grief succumbed to the pain of losing Robert. The room filled to capacity included residents who did not know Robert but shared the heartache with reverence because he was "one of us."

Fifty-seven years having passed, we still miss Robert who was robbed of a full life. No adulthood, no wife, no children, no lifetime accomplishments would come in his name. To us his greatest achievement was being our friend. Having a unique way of bumping up next to a classmate with his fists balled in playful fashion, he always greeted friends in that unique manner which I will always remember.

"Going against the odds" described Robert. A fighter, even with his small frame, he matched up with Thomas Chambers behind the lunchroom one day after lunch. Thomas outweighed Robert by twenty pounds at least. In spite of the physical limitations, he gave Thomas a fierce scrape with Robert receiving a goose egg above his left eye with a bit of blood oozing. But Robert's ferocious swinging and wrestling convinced Thomas he had been in a fight.

At a too-young age, the seventh grade class received a strong testament that life is not fair. Our only respite was to accept it, move on and feel blessed that he had touched our lives. We could thank God for sharing him with us for that brief period at Donalsonville Elementary.

CHAPTER 24

BUCK FEVER

Circa 1959 I was invited to go deer hunting with Great Uncle Gordon Spooner and Daddy. Having never seen a deer in the wild, the thought of taking a shot at one put my head in a spin. Daddy rousted me out about 4:00 a.m. with Uncle Gordon picking us up about 4:30. Buck, his deer hound, was in the back of the truck with his long ears and sad eyes which concealed his excitement of chasing a deer.

Since Uncle Gordon was not kid-friendly, I had concern about being asked and could not understand how this invitation had happened. Probably by putting a "hot bug" in Daddy's ear, Mama had given him the courage to ask Uncle.

Somewhere east of Spring Creek near the old power dam we drove to the house of Coot Covington whose name said it all. With stories to tell about hunting, fishing and other manly pursuits, he struck me as a fascinating man of nature who knew where the deer could be found.

The strategy of hound hunting required putting the dog out near a suspected deer habitat and letting him run the animal toward the hunters posted in a line but separated by only enough distance to prevent a buck from passing through without a shot being fired. Coot posted Uncle Gordon, Daddy and me along a road through the woods where I sat against a pine tree, shivering and hoping that big buck would come my way. Holding my trusty JC Higgins twelve gauge loaded with buck shot, I could picture venison on the table for Christmas.

Soon I heard Buck's mournful bark as he had picked up a scent and was doing his job. With muscles tensing and nerves rattling, I searched the landscape for a deer. Hearing a noise of animals running in the leaves, I judged from the sound that in excess of one had come my way so I imagined nailing multiple bucks.

What a shock I received! Standing thirty feet away I saw three turkeys, Christmas dinner with feathers. By my calculations I could be as great a hero with a turkey or a deer. With no concern for their sex or hunting laws, I had no choice but to shoot. Turkeys were on my "had- not-seen-or-shot" list, also. Sitting there with three turkeys in plain sight and double 0 buckshot in my gun, I realized that a shot to the body would mangle a turkey, leaving only wings, legs and breast pieces which would not complement the dinner table. In a flash of hopeful sheer brilliance, I chose to shoot a turkey in the head to preserve the best parts.

Taking aim, the turkey would not keep its head still for me. Did he not understand that he was posing to die? I tried to follow the head for several seconds and let go of the blast. To my amazement there were three turkeys doing a dance in celebration of my poor strategy, poor aim and general lack of prowess. They appeared to be doing the "Turkey Trot". Remember Little Eva's song back in 1962?

With them taking flight, I pumped two additional shots in their direction, still convinced I was going to shed blood or bag a Christmas table prize. Ever hear a turkey laugh? Not a pleasant sound. Embarrassments like this could turn a young stud into a eunuch. The turkey stayed in the "straw" and I did care.

There would be no wild turkey dinner for Christmas nor hero's welcome from Mama. My brief good graces with Uncle Gordon had expired, probably permanently. He had come to hunt deer, not turkeys, and because of my actions, the deer had disappeared.

That became my one and only deer hunt with me accepting that I would not be invited by Uncle Gordon again. In the coming years, as I thought more about deer hunting, my passion to orphan Bambi dwindled. Hunting doves and quail became my forte. The disrespect from the turkeys had squelched my wild turkey fever.

Finally hunting turkeys again six-seven years ago with my cousin Reuben Roberts, I bagged no gobbler. The best use of my gun came in defending against mosquitoes which were too big to swat. Shot them in the head.

CHAPTER 25

RATTLESNAKE

Seminole County country boys often had encounters with snakes in their youth, an experience yielding an intense drama which is never forgotten. Today I still remember my heart pounding in the back of the throat and feeling dampness in at least one of my shoes.

Circa 1956 Jerome and I had flushed a covey of quail and were searching for the singles. For any rabbits we may have encountered, I carried a twenty-two rifle single shot whereas Jerome had a sixteen gauge Ithaca pump for the quail. As we tromped through the bushes trying to find the quail, walking in single file with big brother in the front, I noticed a pile of circular meat just to my right within two feet of me. Rattlesnake markings, I did not mistake. Yelling, "Snake!" loudly, I brought a sudden halt to our quail hunt.

As I raced like the wind, I unbelievably saw Jerome's hat suspended in mid-air for a second and his gun flying. His flash acceleration had left his hat momentarily where he had digested the fear-invoking word, "snake." What a dumb thing to do, tossing the shotgun! Did Mama raise at least one fool?

Finding a nearby clearing where we gathered our wits, Jerome tried to shoot the snake with my twenty-two. The gun shook so badly that I thought he might be trying to wave it to death. With Jerome taking one shot and missing the target, the snake slithered into the safety of his hole.

In a matter of minutes, accompanied by Daddy with a can of gasoline we returned to the hole and Jerome poured gas down it. Exacting his revenge when the four feet long monster stuck his head out of the hole, Jerome pulled the shotgun trigger blowing off his head. Rattlesnakes, being a common part of the landscape, had to be "reckoned with" since in those days concern for the balance of nature paled in comparison to the perceived need to exterminate the beasts for safety's sake.

Of course, I cannot mention snakes without including the dreaded rattleheadedcoppermoccasin which had been proved to be the most feared of all reptiles. This rare breed, resulting from the cohabitation of copperhead moccasins and rattlesnakes while wintering in the same hole, could disrupt bathroom habits by just mentioning the name. Having never seen one, I had heard the stories relating how vicious and poisonous they could be. I continue to remain on the lookout for the beast.

Over the years a hatred of snakes developed deeply in my psyche, causing warming up to them to not be on my priority list. Nothing could scare this guy more than coiled up death.

CHAPTER 26

SPRING CREEK, BOTTOM UP

Fishing with Great Uncle Luke Spooner and Daddy endures as a compelling childhood memory. Uncle had a circa 1950 Chevrolet pickup truck with the starter and the gear shift in the floor, a vehicle which transported us on fishing trips to either Lake Seminole or Spring Creek, our two fishing locations. Uncle Luke kept it in his barn to block the effects of the elements, but the hibernation from the forces of nature came too late to preserve the medium blue paint which had faded almost beyond detection.

His wooden bateau, twelve feet long and homemade by a relative Kiss Roberts, provided over-the-water transportation. Beginning each fishing trip, Daddy and I loaded the boat into the back of the truck with the tailgate down and secured a spare tire, cut in half across the diameter, underneath the rear end to keep the boat from sliding out.

The workhorse two and one-half horsepower Johnson motor we mounted to a vertical wooden rack on the side of the truck near the driver's side of the cab.

Soon after the Jim Woodruff dam was completed in 1957 creating a 37,500 acre lake, we fished around green trees that had not yet been killed by the water. Being about twelve-thirteen years old, I could not understand the danger when they saw a rain storm threatening. Sometimes the fish bit so well that high wind and rain would threaten to put us in danger. The dead-serious looks on Uncle Luke's and Daddy's faces mirrored the magnitude of their concerns, but the dependable Johnson outboard always returned us to the landing, though at a snail's pace. Possessing no conception of how easily that boat could be swamped, an unforgettable explanation would be forthcoming.

Being such a kind hearted fellow, Uncle Luke will always be missed. He struck a memorable pose with his cigar clenched between his false teeth and his kind eyes smiling. Growing up in a community of relatives such as him and his sweet wife Aunt Delia I feel to be one of life's bonuses. Affectionately referring to her as "the wife" Uncle felt comfortable with that long ago common term of endearment.

Eventually Uncle upgraded to a "speedy" five horsepower Johnson, a major step in technology for my conservative relative. Uncle may not have had the most expensive equipment of the day, but it performed well and gave the three of us great fishing enjoyment.

About July 1959 Uncle Luke, Daddy and I had fished south of US 84 on Spring Creek, caught five-six fish and elected to go north. When we did not catch a lot of fish, they were always biting where we had yet to float our corks so we searched for that prized spot. Uncle was operating his new five horsepower Johnson motor with me on the middle seat and Daddy up front. The move had taken us to about the Ox Hole, just north of the bridge, where Uncle navigated in the center of the creek.

A large runabout with a thirty-five to forty horsepower motor created a big wake when it approached from the rear and came plowing by us. Our boat being pushed from the center of the creek by the wave, Uncle Luke nudged us back to our heading in the middle.

Uncle Luke failed to notice the wake of the big boat as it made its way to both sides of the creek, nor did he take note of the waves rebounding from each bank. But as each lead wave started making its way back to the middle of the creek, he noticed the potential danger and determined that he should take corrective action to ensure the meeting of the waves did not unduly rock the boat. His planned strategy involved speeding up to shoot the front of the boat over the waves. For an excuse later, Uncle pleaded unfamiliarity with the new motor. Accidentally, he had turned the power control in the wrong direction causing the boat to reduce speed and, consequentially, the front to dip down.

Suddenly finding himself accommodating a wave in the front of the boat, Daddy had to think and move fast. This rogue wave would have no part of any negotiations and strongly dictated the terms of what was about to happen as it filled and twisted the boat. Stepping out of the boat into the water, Daddy went to the left and the boat rolled right to left.

The next thing I confronted was coming to the surface under the boat, busy calculating what to do next. The equation being fear + darkness + wet = motivation to find sunshine directed me to the top of the water where I witnessed Uncle Luke floating away with a look of alarm on his face, having set his jaw and pursed his lips. Those lips revealed an accentuated purse since they did not have the support of his false teeth which were in his shirt pocket. With a plastic raincoat in one hand and a life preserver in the other, he floated on a journey down the creek at a good clip.

Luckily, God stepped in and a passenger in the boat ahead had looked back to observe our calamity, so the boat turned around quickly and came back to help. By then Daddy with me hanging on had swum with the overturned boat to the bank. The boat's driver determined we were all right and began to chase Uncle Luke, retrieving him about two hundred yards away at the bridge.

No documented records of freak boating accidents on Spring Creek probably exist. But I would submit that Daddy, Uncle and I were the only ones involved in an overturn caused by the wake of a boat in front of us rebounding off the banks of the creek and precipitated by the boat operator changing speed in the wrong direction.

We gave thanks to our Lord for watching over us that day. All we lost were bait, tackle and fishing paraphernalia, but we kept our lives, resolving again to wear the life jackets, not just to have them in the boat.

CHAPTER 27

HUNTING

With my firing a shotgun for the first time at the age of twelve, a dove in flight crashed from the blast. That first shot from the sixteen gauge pump brought an immediate addiction to the excitement of hunting which became my passion for the next five-six years.

The predilection for hunting came naturally since Daddy and my two older brothers liked the sport. Daddy had about given up hunting when I came along. In his earlier years, shooting game had been not just a sport but a means of putting food on the table. One winter he killed and the family ate seventy-six squirrels from the oaks around Rock Pond with him conserving precious ammo and bringing down two in one shot frequently. Squirrel in a gravy stew fed the family good eatin' for breakfast which complemented cane syrup, biscuits and a helping of grits, the treat causing our taste buds to jump up and down while clapping their hands in harmony.

Peters Victor twelve gauge and sixteen gauge shells cost about two dollars fifty cents, being substantial money in 1957 which would buy nearly a tank of gas. Financing my pursuit was going to take significant effort on my part in our "land of not much money."

Both of my brothers, having jobs at Bartow Gibson's Roadside Milling on Highway 39 with Jerome operating the mobile feed grinder and Lloyd working at the facility, continued living at home during that time. They would hunt on the weekends and leave their left over shells in their hunting jackets at the house. During the week, the shells would disappear when I hunted after school which wore thin after a while.

Recognizing my passion for hunting and the need for ammo, I had to become creative. Having noticed that the wind would blow down corn stalks, making the corn impossible to harvest with the corn picker, I asked Daddy if I could pick up the corn and sell it at Roadside Milling for shell money. He agreed, so I would search the patch and pile up the ears of corn then toss them into the back of the pickup. With corn commanding about a dollar a bushel, five or six bushels provided funds for a couple of boxes of shells. We had one pecan tree for which Mama had lost interest in using the nuts so she allowed me to harvest and sell them.

When I became desperate, Daddy would buy a box of shells. Being familiar with our family not residing on the high end of the income spectrum, I hated to ask.

As with Daddy, hunting became not just a sport for me; putting food on the table added another dimension to the activity. Keeping meticulous records for a year or two, I averaged one dove or quail for every three and a half shells. This computation priced the birds at roughly thirty-five cents each. Wild birds were expensive next to cubed steak and pork chops but a welcome treat for us who loved wild meat. Stewed dove or quail with gravy poured over rice and biscuits delivered chow time heaven.

As trained by Lloyd, I developed a habit of always cleaning what I killed which put me in charge of plucking the doves or skinning the quail, removing the entrails and presenting the birds to Mama. She would always check them again picking out bird shot and removing pin feathers from the dove that I would have missed. Being impossible for her and me to find all the bird shot, the family ate some of them.

Fifteen or so years back, I was x-rayed for a diagnosis, and a bird shot pellet showed up on the film. When the technician asked me what the tiny speck could be, I had to think a minute before declaring it to be lead. Usually the birdshot passed right through but this one had gotten temporarily stuck.

My time after school days and on Saturdays during the fall and winter was mostly spent in the woods or fields. Of course, if Daddy needed help, that was always a priority, but work always decreased on the farm during this time of year. On a typical Saturday, I would leave our house walking with our senior Irish setter Jack when I first started hunting and later with my pit bull Chief. The dog and I would head out through Great Uncle Bud Youmans's woods in front of our house.

Trekking through better than a mile of woods usually yielded a couple of coveys of quail. Familiarity with the birds feeding areas produced a notion of where every covey was likely to be. The dog would help me flush them, so I would shoot two or three on the covey rise and watch where the singles landed. Proceeding in that direction, I would roust the singles and bag additional birds.

The destination of the long walk would be Cousin Frank Spooner's waterhole which was about two miles from our house. The habitat possessed the right features for attracting doves. The waterhole being surrounded by clean pasture and having no brush or tall weeds made it easier for doves to watch for hawks, their natural predator. The water hole's grey clay bottom caused it to hold water well, so I had never seen it dry.

Having a rich history, Cousin Frank fought in WWI and once told a story of fighting in wheat fields that involved bullets clipping the wheat around him. He was a tough guy who was married to Cordelia, a fine lady, who used words stingily but made a strong point when she spoke.

Knowing that Mr. Frank dearly loved the birds, I would take four-six dove for him and his wife to enjoy and to show appreciation for hunting on his land.

When I think of him, I always remember a huge, magnificent oak tree that had distinguished itself years before by growing in the middle of the dirt road in front of their house causing drivers to go around it, but progress dictated it should be cut down when the road was paved.

Shooting doves around water created a special difficulty with retrieving the kills. The unwritten rule, dictating that a hunter retrieve game wherever it fell, created a problem when a dove landed in the water. At first being a novice, I would just wade in my boots which resulted in chilly feet on the two-mile walk back home. This discomfort necessitated my discovering a better, obvious solution — my waiting for the wind to blow the downed bird to the edge.

Having heard my brother speak of taking two doves in one shot, I figured that could be done by me as well. When two doves flew together, a hunter could watch carefully for them to cross as they flew by. Pulling the trigger at that instant would bring down two at a time. Successfully doing this several times made me feel like being a better shot than I actually was.

During those times alone in the woods, I never encountered a rattlesnake. Having dealt with rattlesnakes four times — twice with Daddy, once with my first cousin and once with my brother, my unpleasant incidents with rattlers had thankfully ended.

While dove hunting and walking around the edge of a swampy area, I noticed this thick blackish snake in the middle of where my next step would be, simultaneously hearing a loud hissing sound. Breathing deliberately, I carefully backed up three or four steps and shot from the hip to eliminate the time required to move the weapon to my shoulder. The blast hit the mud beneath the snake and blew him about two feet into the air to my dismay. Now I had this wiggling mass of snake in the air in front of me. Not what I wanted! When he hit the ground, I fired two extra times and missed as he headed deeper into the swamp. I directed my feet toward dry ground.

Now fully realizing the dangers, I should not have been in the woods without a friend. Being at least a mile from help a portion of the time, one bite from a poisonous snake could have brought the family together and earned me a marker in Rock Pond Cemetery. I advise strongly against hunting alone because snakes are only one possible danger.

In my teen years, girls did not fit into my plans; they cost money of which I was eternally short. On Friday and Saturday nights, Daddy gave me fifty cents when I headed to town on the truck. Stretching that as I could, entertaining a girlfriend did not enter my world of possibilities. Hunting I wisely viewed as cheaper, counting on the availability of time in the future to bag the prized love of my life — and I did.

CHAPTER 28

ADVENTURES WITH JIMMY

Jimmy Williams is a first cousin with his mother Iris being Mama's sister, so from the age of about twelve, he and I spent a lot of time together on the weekends and in the summer. We always respected each other and had plenty of good times without the electronic miracles of today such as cell phones, lap tops, computer games and other similar devices. Possessing imaginations and a love of being in nature, we stayed busy year round.

Chasing rabbits with my pit bull Chief was an active, rousing adventure every time. Neither hot nor cold weather hampered us or Chief when we had a yearning to run a bunny. The best part of the chase was watching Chief who loved to chase the furry critters. If a rabbit happened to frequent thick, tall weeds, Chief would jump four-five feet into the air and search for a brief moment to spot which direction ol' Bugs was headed. Jimmy and I did not especially care if we bagged the critter with our recognizing that Chief, the woods and the excitement of the chase had all the kicks. We would often take one home to feed our cats, our family having a population of as many as eighteen on the farm at one time.

My older brothers fought wasps, and so did Jimmy and I, breaking china berry limbs and looking for a nest. An old, abandoned sharecropper house next door was always loaded with wasps for entertainment and excitement. The Guinea wasps, being prevalent, offered many fierce battles with casualties on both sides.

Jimmy or I would toss a rock or stick at the nest, stirring them up and bringing them at full speed, brandishing stingers. The chinaberry limbs and our fast feet provided our defenses. Being agile, we usually avoided the stingers, but eventually the underdogs could not be denied their prize – a stinger inserted in a neck, arm or on the head. Stinging did not bother us since we had been bitten so often that our bodies were at least partially immune to the effects of the poison. Jimmy and I did not stop the battle until the nest was torn down.

There were three strategies for dealing with those buggers: swatting them, retreating and retreating while swatting them.

The larger red wasps presented a completely different opposition. Those fellows carried a tank load of poison and knew how to pop it to us, their stingers hurting powerfully and yielding significant swelling. Also, red wasps chased farther, once trying to open the screen door after we had retreated to the house during one ferocious encounter. Lucky for us, we had hooked the latch.

My brother Lloyd had given me a Daisy pump air rifle for Christmas. When a young boy received an air rifle, he had to wage war on something, field wrens being our favorite prey. Wrens, being plentiful and preferring to hang around the hog feeders, Jimmy and I would lie in wait to ambush them when they came to feed.

With only one gun, we took turns, so one of us took shots then passed the gun to the other. Keeping count, Jimmy and I would shoot ten-twenty a day, providing food for the cats. In Iron City an older gentleman ate robins, so we would take him a supply on occasions.

Slaying birds with BB guns was part of the culture in the '50s. Today, I would view the activity very differently.

Hanging out with the "Iron City Gang," including Joe Ard, Donald Heath, Wellborn Settles, Kenneth Sanders and Bill Bainbridge, came to be a way to spend a Saturday or Sunday. The group would sometimes organize a softball or basketball game, or we might spend time sitting on the Iron City Depot porch shooting the breeze while watching the traffic pass through on U.S. 84.

With me having a bicycle that was still functional, Jimmy and I would alternate pedaling and riding on the handle bars. Once we rode three miles to the Buckhole where we found our friend Buddy Odom. On a whim we three swam naked in the water at the Fish Pond Drain Bridge, a joy which ended abruptly when a car came along, and we all scrambled for clothes. As we jerked our clothes on, precious twenty-two rifle cartridges unexpectedly fell in the water – oh the price of fun!

Now we had to pedal the bicycle three miles home. The handle bars could really wear on a young fellow's butt, ours being boney already since Jimmy and I both were rail thin.

Camping out in the middle of a field on our farm offered a fine way to spend a Friday or Saturday night in the summer. Using a twenty-two rifle, a flashlight and Jimmy's old Army tent, which was just the right size for us, and supported by Chief who slept outside we had protection from the elements and varmints.

Staying up for the night and accompanying Chief on several rabbit chases included loads of excitement and fun. Heading out into the dark with flash lights and following Chief's bark, we tromped all over our fifty acres. With rabbits being difficult to get in the dark, we only bagged some exercise.

Having been up about the entire night and being dead tired the next day, I had to be sure Daddy had no work planned because I needed to find a soft bed to catch up with sleep.

One day as we walked in the woods, a rattlesnake, lying adjacent to a dead rabbit with blood running out of one of his eyes, appeared under a hardwood tree. On the verge of swallowing his feast, the reptile started crawling away as fast as he could. But Jimmy and I followed with my single shot twenty-two and cancelled his ticket.

We loved an old marshy pond deep in the woods and would walk around it hoping to stir up whatever. Jimmy was up ahead of me, so as I walked the edge, on the way to the water a sizeable water moccasin crossed my path only a foot or two ahead. Learning a lesson, I tried to never again intrude between a water moccasin and the water.

Our fun always was getting interrupted by responsibilities. To have veggies during the year, food had to be stored in the freezer every summer. After our mule died, Daddy would cultivate the garden with the tractor, planting large gardens of black-eyed peas, purple hull peas, butter beans, tomatoes, snap beans, potatoes and okra. Iris, his mother, and Jimmy would come to our house, and we four worked to gather, shell, blanch and freeze the peas and beans.

The first thing in the morning we picked the vegetables. Then, for hours we would sit under a mimosa tree, listening to the radio while watching the flesh on our thumbs prune up and wear away from shelling peas or beans. Mama and Aunt Iris could talk extensively, but we fought boredom and sore thumbs in a big way.

When it came time to freeze a supply of field corn, we picked it from our crop in the fields since sweet corn found in stores was anathema to our taste buds. We filled wash tubs with corn in the morning then went to our house to shuck and remove the silks under a chinaberry tree; Mama and Aunt Iris handled the grating and packaging for freezing.

Field corn remains as the best tasting corn I have ever eaten. Why this wonderful tasting food is not widely offered in food stores stands as an amazement to me.

While Mama and Aunt Iris were grating, we went to the barn yard, located a stick to use for a bat and began knocking corn cobs, alternating pitching and hitting. Neither of us owned a baseball or softball, nor a bat. With meager items to work with, we could always create a way to generate some fun.

Lloyd had made "horse shoes" in Agriculture class which were only iron rods bent into a U shape. With two stakes driven in the ground, we could play horse shoes. Somehow during a game, one landed in the chinaberry tree with Jimmy volunteering to climb up to retrieve it. As he crawled out on the limb and was about to grab it, the limb broke. Down came Jimmy, the horse shoe and a sizeable chinaberry limb. Trying to cushion the fall with one of his hands, he yelled while revealing that one of his wrists did not look normal and exhibited a big hump. Sharing choice words with him on the way there and on the way home, Aunt Iris drove him to the doctor to get it set and have a cast applied.

The best enjoyment we had at ages fifteen-sixteen involved dove shoots. A relative Raymond Simmons had productive fields for doves after the corn harvest. A drainage ditch which provided cover ran through the middle of the best field. The doves would come out of Cousin Bud Youmans's woods and fly across the field in droves making it possible for Jimmy and me to leave with a full bag about every time. Saturday afternoons during dove season would always find us enjoying the sport of hunting.

When we were shooting doves in a harvested peanut patch adjacent to my Great Uncle Carl Spooner's house, misfortune came calling. Understanding that one day a game warden would try to ruin a hunt, my hunting routine required me to keep an accurate count of the doves in my bag. Today my mental tally said that I had fourteen which were two past the limit.

Being positioned roughly thirty yards from Uncle Carl's barn and equipment sheds, suddenly I saw a green pickup coming down the road with insignia on the side. Sprinting toward the sheds which were between me and the advancing truck, I dropped two doves along the way in the weeds. The warden became disturbed by my behavior as he came driving fast up the lane to Uncle's house.

Nonchalantly, I walked toward him when he stopped and stepped out of his truck. With a stern look on his face, he demanded to hear why I was running. Thinking fast, I told him that I had shot a bird down and was chasing him. Sprouting a frown, he checked my gun for a plug, checked my license and started counting the birds in my bag. There I stood, quaking in my boots, wondering if I had counted correctly. Relief swarmed over me when he pulled out the twelfth one, thereby emptying the bag.

What a close call! With this incident being the only time a game warden had checked me, I had to consider what the law did with a young boy who could not pay his fine? Asking him, never came to my mind.

Jimmy, who lives on Lake Lanier near Gainesville, Georgia, still visits with me on the phone and infrequently we see each other. From background and heritage standpoints, I have more in common with him than anyone except my wife. Jim has always been a loyal friend and cousin with whom I was fortunate to make lasting memories that I genuinely cherish.

We always laugh when we hear of a young person being bored because we realized that boredom did not come our way when we were young, except during those times of shelling peas and beans under the mimosa tree.

CHAPTER 29

IN A PICKLE

The summer of 1957 had me working at my Great Uncle and Aunt's egg operation down the road from our house. Being twelve years old, I was ready for my first public job which included assisting Rudolph Shores with feeding chickens, gathering eggs and packaging them.

Having known them since I was old enough to remember what was going on in the world, Uncle Bud and Aunt Lila Mae Youmans had always been family to me. I came to know the Youmans children as they were added to the brood, including in order of birth Gus, Susan, Jody, Bob and Judy. None of the children were much more than a year apart in age, so all but Judy romped over the yards and the egg operation area that August.

Utilizing a Ford 8N tractor, pulling a flatbed trailer, in the feeding of the poultry and harvesting of the eggs, Rudolph and I agreed that when the tractor was started, the driver needed to know the locations of the children. Often they begged for rides, but we chose to avoid that charge. Bob and Jody, about two and three years old respectively, had a difficult time understanding the word "no" and took free reign of their large roaming area.

As the routine dictated, at 3:00 or 4:00 p.m. daily, Rudolph told me to pull the tractor and trailer in between the chicken houses to begin the feeding process. The tractor had a button starter which required pushing to crank the engine with a vertical gear shift conveniently adjacent to the starter.

Habitually performing a scan of the area for any kids, I observed that Bob and Jody stood an appreciable distance away of twenty-thirty feet. My finger depressed the starter, so in seconds the engine came alive with me reaching deftly to the gear stick, jerking it into gear and starting to raise my foot from the clutch. As I lifted the foot, my peripheral vision detected the images of Bob and Jody out of the corner of my left eye. In a flash Bob had positioned himself inside the path of the left wheel, and Jody stood in front of the tractor tire, looking up as if to want a ride.

A wave of terror coursed its way through my body and to my brain. As I moved my left rubber boot, coated in chicken manure, back down on the clutch, it slipped. Making another motion toward planting my foot solidly on the clutch, I successfully pushed it down. In that brief instant, the tractor had traveled five or six feet knocking Bob to the ground with the axle and out of harm's way and pushing Jody down with the tractor wheel rolling across his back, face down.

To my total astonishment and with God's mercy, Jody jumped up and ran several feet from the tractor to let out a crying scream. My heart must have skipped several beats as I watched this horror because children are usually critically or mortally wounded when incurring such trauma. Nevertheless, I am witnessing Jody, possibly okay, but expressing his fright, distress and pain. Rudolph, having seen the accident, grabbed Jody in one motion and headed for the house to find Aunt Lila Mae.

With my world in a spin, I stepped down from the tractor, attempting to regain my senses, realizing an unbelievable misfortune had just happened with me being the one responsible.

A recollection of the past flashed through my brain. Rudolph had nicknamed Jody, "Joker." Being a skinny three year old with a delightful smile and hopefully a full life ahead of him, Joker had just been placed in grave danger.

As I observed the spot and noticed interrupted tractor marks in the dirt where Jody had been lying, I determined that the dirt in the spot was soft and wet. The cushioning of the unpacked dirt along with his young age were the two positives that made a big difference in the outcome of the casualty.

By the time I had walked to the house, Aunt Lila Mae had put Jody in the station wagon and was headed out of the driveway. So terribly I hated to face her when she returned, hopefully bearing good news. Waiting in the Youmans' day room with Brycie, a maid that helped with the children and house work, every minute seemed an hour long. How desperately I wanted news that Jody would be all right.

Two or three hours had passed when the station wagon pulled back into the driveway, and Aunt Lila Mae walked into the house. Being in a quiet, serious state of mind, she told me that the doctor thought the only damage was massive bruising. He was being kept overnight for observation, but she was optimistic that he would be just fine.

Trying to express my deep sorrow, the words came out haltingly and not making sense as I would have preferred. Aunt Lila Mae was gracious and understanding, but with me possessing enormous regret only a big slap from her could have made me feel better.

The small Ford tractor had exerted at least 300-400 pounds of force to the young tike's back. God had taken care of us that day and prevented Jody and me from enduring a dreadful pickle.

Having not seen Jody in twelve or so years, I understand that he is retired from a construction company where he had worked for years and now involved in farming in the county. Seeing or thinking about him is impossible without mentally going back to that awful day. At a recent Spooner family reunion, I mentioned the incident to Susan who said that she had never heard the details of what really happened. This bit of prose is to inform her, Bob, Gus, Jody and Judy of what really transpired that long ago day.

CHAPTER 30

SEMINOLE COUNTY HIGH SCHOOL

In September 1958 one hundred eighteen students from Donalsonville, Iron City and FDR elementary schools arrived at SCHS to begin the eighth grade. Unable to describe the phenomenon at the time, we participated in a culture clash. About fifteen to twenty-five percent of the students came from each of the two smaller schools and the rest from the Donalsonville elementary school. A small number of kids from one of those smaller schools liked to fight and bully contributing to the troublemakers' failing grades and inability to complete high school. Life has a way of sorting things out. Below are a portion of the memorable happenings of the five years:

PE

Playing soccer or rag football in shorts and t-shirts when the temperature of 40 degrees had zero appeal. What were the coaches thinking when they concluded that this was a healthy activity? In today's world, it would be child abuse. The smart ones participated vigorously to warm up and maintain body heat.

Horseshoes

I had never played horse shoes nor gambled on the sport, but the game, on the south side of the gym where guys lost their lunch money, became an attraction. Trying to hustle the new kids on the block, the seniors thought they had some pigeons, but no one dominated regardless of their age or size. Larry Chance, being a devotee, tossed shoes but did not take me to the cleaners since eating lunch was my high priority.

Cracker Balls

Cracker balls, small explosives about half the size of a marble, generated mischief. When stepped on, they would explode, causing a loud mini boom that disrupted class changes while frustrating the teachers and principal trying to catch the offenders. Dropping cracker balls in the hall during movement to the next class constituted the perfect crime. Having holes in their pockets, the instigators dribbled them down their pants legs as they walked in a crowd. BANG! POW! POW! Everyone laughed when students jumped high from the sound beneath their feet.

Apple Blossom Perfume

A joker determined that it would be a kick to pour this obnoxious substance called Apple Blossom Perfume on the radiators. With the heat enhancing the smell, the building had this awful smell floating throughout. The administrators could not nab the culprits, but the students had accurate suspicions.

Tenth Grade English

Margaret Daniels, having started her teaching career at SCHS, presented our class the obligation of breaking her in right. Coming prepared with a paddle, she made students wonder about its purpose since we were all darlings.

My cuz Reuben Roberts and I were whispering, unfortunately choosing the wrong day in Mrs. Daniels' cycle, which provoked her to whip out that paddle from her desk drawer and request an audience with us in the front of the room. Having relieved her stress on both of us, we resolved to whisper very quietly in the future. Afterward, I seriously considered placing Midol on her desk, when she was not present, to calm her down in that tense part of the month. Today I occasionally see her in a restaurant or at a class reunion and razz her about that vicious beating with a piece of wood.

Biology

One of our coaches taught biology class or at least sat at the desk in the front of the room. Unfortunately, he could not distinguish an amoeba from a school bus. Possessing a unique teaching style, he would have us read, in rotation, from the book. Concluding that he sorely lacked in knowledge of the subject, we hesitated to ask questions since he had no foggy clue of a response. His memorable flub, pronouncing the word "phlegm" phonetically as "flegem" brought subdued laughter from students who recognized the mistake. From the time the bell rang the first time until it rang the second, the county's tax dollars were not at work. They were resting.

Rat Snake

Bringing a rat snake to school in a glass jar for a science class exhibit, my buddy Glen Hill destroyed class decorum. Being in world history class with Miss Pitts, when he elected to remove the lid, and pull the rat snake out to tantalize the students, a shocking calamity unfurled. As rat snakes will do, he put a kink in his body, and Glen could not return him to the jar, a feat requiring him to pull the snake all the way out to reinsert him. At this point happenstance and nature took control with the snake developing a sudden need to make potty. In seconds he had dumped green, foul smelling excrement all over the floor putting Glen in the janitorial business when Miss Pitts ordered him to clean the floor. The class roared and Glen fell, perhaps irretrievably, out of her graces.

Passing Gas

In the same world history class, I sat behind a girl who must have had beans three times a day precipitating a foul smell rising frequently which would burn my nostrils. Experiencing an overwhelming battle of tolerance every day, I determined that God was testing me, but I had passed, almost passed out several times.

Love in Bloom

I cannot remember the details of why this happened, but Terry Ingram and John Ray Stout were both involved with a girl. John Ray, being the hot tempered one, had plans of whipping Terry's ass. Doubts of his sanity were rampant since Terry had him by two years, outweighed him by twenty-five or thirty pounds and was a couple of inches taller. Choosing a site for their altercation to the left of the front steps of the school and about thirty feet from the principal's office, they squared off and started swinging. After only three-four licks being passed, Mr. Jenkins broke up the fight with John Ray muffling a sigh of relief as his head was about to get pounded terribly.

Gambling

In an Einstein moment, guys rolling dice chose the steps just outside an entrance to a gym locker room to do their deed. Having a grand old time tossing those bones, the merriment ended when suddenly the door opened and out walked Mr. Jenkins. Being astonished, the boys knew they were about to have church when words get really serious and smiles go into hibernation. Marching solemnly behind the principal, the group headed to the principal's office suspecting the bad news of their parents having to make an unplanned trip to town.

Fighting

Larry "Deadeye" Odom, always looking for a fight, found his share. Choosing the wrong guy to confront one afternoon resulted in a severe butt kicking being dropped on him. What a shock for Deadeye! David Jones like Bill Elliot in the cowboy westerns chose the role of a "peaceable man" with no fights on his card to that point. For an unknown reason, one day in the parking lot Larry took a swing at David who unleashed a plethora of swinging fists. Apparently having never fought a southpaw, Deadeye lacked technique for defending against David's left hand which left him exposed to every blow. David swung his left hand skillfully and pounded him almost to the "hot furnace" below.

Larry delighted in the fight ending when David became tired and walked away proud of delivering the devil his due. Good job, David! God rest his soul.

Being brief, but poignant, another fight lacked flare. Walking to the flag pole in front of the school after classes had finished for the day, Buddy Odom and Eugene Davis had determined that they did not like each other. Causing no damage, they took several swings at each other with both breathing that proverbial sigh of relief. Eugene began his stroll home down the street, and Buddy walked away to wait for his bus. What a boring fight!

Cuban Missile Crisis

When JFK invoked the Monroe Doctrine and demanded that Khrushchev remove the missiles from Cuba, fear took hold of our nation. The students' unsettled psyches came to Mrs. Dorothy Dale's American History class. Displaying an amazing ability to connect with the class, she explained what was happening and tried to allay our fears. Thank God Krushchev blinked and the missiles were removed. The thought of being cremated while hiding under my desk sounded like an unappealing way to check out.

Rowdy Locker Room

After PE one day, the din in the locker room reached a stereophonic level. Taking showers and getting dressed the class ignored the volume because it sounded like a familiar level which had been achieved before. What was the problem? Guessing that Coach Daniels felt anxious because of lack of attention at home, we were unaffected when he asked who made the noise and became perturbed. As always, we knew that Buz Guterman and Bill Bainbridge loved their roles as perpetrators, but no one ratted, maintaining the code of silence.

As we left the locker room the next day, each of us received two whacks with a paddle being not exactly what I would call an intervention or a behavior changer. It probably made the coach feel better.

Study Hall

Why they called it study hall, I will never understand. Three types of kids attended study hall: those who would not study, those who did not need to study and students that studied. Heading to the library, the derelicts tried to extract the last drop of patience and understanding from the librarian Mrs. Kirkland who was such a sweet, loving woman whom I can only remember with warm thoughts. I read the magazines with the pictures, especially "Life" and its articles documenting life of the times, and tried to keep my mouth shut.

Ann Smith

From the first day this teacher was all business, whereas her demeanor communicated that jerking her chain included hanging from it. Being effective, she maintained order in her room, not having to ask for it often. The demanding look in her eye communicated that I would learn English in her class. Capable of writing English today, I defy anyone reared in the South to divest themselves of speaking with the run together words, ain't, fixin' to, and a variety of other expressions of red neck English. Language habits learned in our youth stay with us and why should they not? They were part of our raisin'.

SCHS provided a sound education during my awkward years, as graduating brought a tremendous sense of accomplishment and relief. A math teacher Mrs. Mervis Bridges asked us to share what we intended to do with our work lives near the end of the twelfth grade. Incapable of thinking of another alternative at the time and not wanting to weird out by being silent, I told of plans to get a job in the postal service.

Two years after high school, I took the SAT, the scores setting me up for my first year at Abraham Baldwin Agricultural College. The next year I transferred to Georgia Tech, finishing in 1970 with a Bachelor of Industrial Engineering Degree. With the degree I set about gaining restitution for those hard years in poverty — and I did.

CHAPTER 31

DENS OF INEQUITY

In the '50s and '60s, there were two pool rooms in town, Ed's and Charlie's which shared equally in their attempt to pervert my latter teen years. Daddy played pool, both brothers played, so destiny had control as my driver license became a permit for venturing into the "dens of inequity".

Having a dark stigma attached, the rooms were male bastions and never frequented by the female sex. If a woman or girl wanted to see someone inside, they stood at the door until the party was found and came to them.

Ed's was larger with elevated chairs for observing the action with five-six pool tables and two snooker tables. Charlie's had less elaborate furnishings, about three-four pool tables and one snooker table. The pee trough in Charlie's with its acrid smells and the room's rustic appearance added charm and ambience to an already atmosphere-rich environment. Both attracted players in numbers on Saturdays causing temporary waits for a table at times.

Open wagering on six ball, nine ball, snooker and check dominated the rooms with clouds of cigarette smoke and four letter words topping off the setting. Having been around Daddy's Prince Albert for years, smoking did not bother me other than irritating my throat after putting in a long shift leaning over the tables.

The preponderance of four letter words spilling forth when a hot player missed a straight-in shot added to the din with guys getting loud when losing their money. The use of the pool cue, an extension of the brain, only turned worse when the nerves frayed, making "cool" the best strategy, though I must confess to never mastering the art.

There were loads of personalities who frequented the places: Ed Miller, Larry Batchelor, Irving Herring, Lamar Hicks, Peyton Horne, Buddy Odom, Buz Guterman, Chris "Rabbit" Gibbons, Wallace Shivers, Steve Holt and Leroy Lewis to name a slice of the well-seasoned faithful.

Watching and listening to Ed Miller, worth a spectator paying admission, as he attracted an audience when he reached a mellow level of inebriation. Ed's bulk, in the neighborhood of three hundred pounds, resulted in a guy kidding him one day who said, "Ed, looks like you have put on a few pounds." Ed responded, "I guess by God I have. They said I weighed eight pounds when I was born."

Irving Herring could shoot harder and straighter than anyone, always assaulting the cue ball which often jumped the table and rolled on the floor prompting players to ask, "Do you want to play pool or marbles?"

Wallace and Steve, adjoining-county residents, came to Donalsonville to get an education in the skills of pool for which they paid dearly. Taking their lumps, eventually they improved, becoming formidable opponents to the point that cash outflows and inflows nearly equalized.

My strong suspicions said that Leroy had made Ed's his home since he was always there when I arrived and left.

Buz and Chris nursed a strong ongoing rivalry with one always owing the other a tab in a seemingly cashless competition. No one knows who got the better of that competition with both proclaiming dominance. Let's just say that neither took an around the world cruise on the winnings, but they both shot a mean stick.

Chris, of a unique genre, could handle a stick effortlessly and possessed an innate ability to cuss loud and shoot straight at the same time. When a car that he was working under fell from a jack, Chris's forearms both broke between the elbows and wrists, a twist of fate which resulted in his game being the best ever during recuperation. Casts on both arms, stroking the cue like a pro, with that ever present cig hanging out of his mouth, he struck the perfect anti-choirboy pose.

My friend Buddy Odom had a steer that won reserve grand champion in 1962. After paying his feed bill, Buddy pocketed about fifty dollars. Since he owed me money, Buddy agreed to back me in a game of six ball with him playing, also. On the surface the arrangement should have given us an edge; nevertheless, we walked out with the bulk of his money in other guys' pockets. Appearances dictated that we had encountered a "bum steer."

Playing six ball often attracted five or six players at a time with the game being won and a portion of the players not getting a shot. Usually the competitors bet a quarter a game. Getting his cut, Ed charged ten cents a game per player, so guess who made the real money.

On occasions I walked into the pool room at twelve noon and walked out at midnight getting my nourishment chiefly from orange sodas and Lance cheese crackers, adding packs of Tom's Toasted Peanuts to balance the diet. On a lucky day, I exited the establishment with ten dollars plus in my jeans which beat the embarrassment of having to sneak to my car wearing only undershorts. Having over ten dollars made a guy feel borderline rich.

I fondly remember the enjoyment, the incidents, the characters and the lessons learned in Ed's and Charlie's pool rooms. In a warped way, those days contributed to my education in life helping round me out as a young adult. Never again did gambling peak my interest since owning a healthy appreciation for family and hard-earned money erected a strong barrier against betting money on games of skill or luck.

CHAPTER 32

THE TANGERINE CAPER

A teenager, not always understanding exactly why he does what he does, can commit dumb acts when looking for entertainment or waging a war against boredom. In retrospect, fifty-two years after the stupidity, with the fog having lifted, I understand clearly that the taking of tangerines without permission occurred for the sake of the adventure and was not about the fruit. The adventure, carrying a huge bill for my conscience, brought a wagon load of strife. If I could have only stopped for a minute and considered the consequences, painful stress and self-examination could have been avoided. No, that is not what seventeen year olds do; they just do as if life had no repercussions.

It all started with my ol' pal Buddy Odom and me sitting around bored. Thinking unclearly, I mentioned that I knew the location of trees containing the world's sweetest tangerines. Those words set a snowball of turmoil rolling, moving me and the attached consequences downhill with no hope of applying the brakes.

Our plan involved parking my '53 Studebaker down the road, sneaking through a cow pasture to the back of the house and helping ourselves. The first trip was uneventful. However, Buddy did receive a scare when we were walking under an oak tree and a twig caught his shirt in the back near his neck and shoulder. Being hyper anxious and vulnerable to unplanned events, Buddy thought he had been caught in the execution of a crime. Jumping sideways, he balled his fists and said, "Turn me loose, you son of a bitch." Walking behind him and seeing it happen in the moonlight brought forth a need to roar with laughter, but I had to place my hand on my mouth to maintain silence. His unanticipated reaction to a phantom arm of justice nearly snapped my funny bone. A twig had caught him. An omen had dropped in our laps, but we did not recognize it.

Collecting our bounty of a dozen or so tangerines, we headed back to the Tastee Freeze to savor them with friends. The twig, trying to apprehend him, kept coming up causing laughter tears to flow down my cheeks.

The next week we went back, picking a dozen plus, getting cocksure and thinking nobody would miss them from the tree. Without knowledge that this senior widow, having identified the loss, had begun plotting with her son to bring our night time forays to a rubber-burning halt, we thought our next trip would be unnoticed as well.

Not many days thereafter, we saw Bob Dutton and Harry Cobb at the Tastee Freeze. We sat around shooting the breeze for a while, and the subject of tangerines lifted its nasty head. Deciding that we had an appetite for some tasty tangerines, we all jumped into the Studebaker and motored to the dirt road by the house with the trees.

Buddy, Bob and Harry intended to gather the fruit, and I would wait in the car. To me it sounded like a fine plan since I perceived my risk would be less driving the getaway car. Considering a person might drive by and see the parked vehicle, I planned to drive down the road and come back to get them when they had finished the deed.

As they scampered across a pasture and circled to get a rear-entrance access to the tangerine trees, something happened which we had no way of anticipating. A loud explosion from a blasting cap or a stick of dynamite shook the ground and lit up the cow pasture. Also, it set Buddy, Bob and Harry "on fire" who scattered like chickens with a hawk in tow.

We learned the following week that the widow's son was a demolition expert in WWII and had placed a trip wire that would cause the explosives to ignite. If we had known of his expertise, we would have found other amusement that night. One of my friends had stumbled over the trap resulting in more surprises to come.

Headed down the road while hoping the guys could get back, I spotted Buddy who jumped into the car. Bob and Harry had disappeared or at least they had tried to vanish. Were they shell shocked? Where did they go? Were they injured? They were probably not hurt unless they had been injured climbing over or running through barbed wire fences.

Buddy and I cruised on back to the Tastee Freeze while asking ourselves where Bob and Harry could be. Thirty to forty-five minutes later, they were still missing.

Then I saw a sight that was the picture of dread. Daddy drove up in his pickup truck, accompanied by the widow's son in his vehicle. The son had gone to our house and awakened Daddy generating my worst nightmare, which I could not end by waking and turning over. Suspecting the son had convinced Daddy that I was stealing his mother's tangerines that night, I had to think and talk fast. Could it get any worse?

Stepping out of my car, I walked over to them minus the cheery greetings and sensed we were going to have a church revival in the Tastee Freeze parking lot. The son began applying a strong effort to have me admit trying to steal the tangerines with Daddy's face ostensibly begging for a helping of the truth and a side dish of misunderstanding. I pleaded innocent to being a part of tangerine theft that night; nevertheless, I admitted to being out on the road with my car, aware that it had been seen. There was no way that I could tell Daddy the complete, unvarnished truth in front of that guy; my tongue, lips and mouth refused to form the words.

Daddy knew me well enough to understand that my version lacked total credibility, doubting that I had passed on the truthful version. With them getting into their trucks and heading home, my heart took a troubled shot at regaining its natural rhythm.

Minutes afterward, Bob and Harry arrived at the Tastee Freeze, tired from a two mile moonlight walk and run through the countryside. They had climbed many fences, navigating toward the bright lights of the hangout. After filling them in on the evening's events, we had a mild laugh on my part and stronger one on theirs with the dread of the next morning moving to the center of my thoughts. Their dads were not pulled out of a deep sleep to be told their son was a thief, so their tomorrow mornings would be no different.

Confronting Mama the next morning was tougher than Daddy. With a sad, disappointed look, she calmly told me how badly she felt about what she thought had transpired. So low that I could have walked under a snake's belly and not even mussed my hair, sensing unequaled shame, I could not make eye contact.

Daddy felt compelled to compare me to my brothers, "They did bad stuff but they never stole anything." The best decision for me was to stand there and take it, realizing that silence would mitigate the confrontation. Obviously, Daddy had an incomplete knowledge of the mischief my brothers had done during their carousing, or he would have chosen a different tact.

Mama had received a letter from the widow several days afterward, and she asked me to read it, her way of further dousing me in the consequences. I knew she and Mama had been friends and distant cousins to that point since I had been on visits to her house with Mama. She attacked the extended family and recounted a relative way up the family tree who had stolen and declared that I was going to have a similar life of crime. To her, calling me lizard bait would have been a compliment, since I merited worse.

I retired from my life of crime after that fiasco, giving up pillaging and looting the countryside and making everyone's fruit in their back yards safe. My picture would never be with an article in a newspaper, detailing arrests, police chases or other law enforcement actions.

The poor judgment gifted me with the worst bout of conscience of my young life. Luckily, my wayward incident occurred in my youth which secured my moral future by my solemn commitment to never bear that kind of disappointment again. Awareness of the impropriety, but transgressing anyhow, triggered the storage of long term memory, deep in my grey matter, to remind me of the importance of doing the right thing. Those were scrumptious tangerines, though.

CHAPTER 33

WHITE COLLAR JOB

In January 1963 I began my first "white collar job" at the new **Piggly Wiggly** in Donalsonville. The bagboy job was the first work which did not leave me hog-dirty at the end of the day. Compared to the work I had been doing on the farm, it was a piece of cake. My buddy Terry Ingram had put in a word for me, and Mama had made a plea so I had received word to be there at 6:00 a.m.

My sister had recently given me a 1953 Studebaker, nicknamed the "Rutabaga," when her husband passed away. The job would provide gas and other needed mechanical attention to keep me mobile. The car companies do not make cars like that anymore: praise the Lord.

A couple of friends of mine and I were bumping down a dirt road one afternoon after school, and I hit a larger than usual bump. The rear end of the car started making a whining, grinding noise. I pulled over and looked under the car to see if everything was still in place. Getting back in, I told my friends that it was the differential. It continued making that roaring sound until the day I sold it for one hundred twenty-five dollars. Sucker!

Every Saturday the workday kicked off with bagboys in the back storage room bagging potatoes with ten pounds to the bag. Being the largest pile of potatoes I had seen in my life, I thought that our family's potatoes spread on the floor in the barn seemed like a tiny pile when compared to the quantity we bagboys packaged.

After the potatoes, setting up a display of Nabisco saltine crackers demanded my attention. This was my first opening to impress the boss so I meticulously began constructing the "Empire State Building" of saltines. As I reached about chest high with the boxes, Terry walked by and said, "You know, you have to put price stickers on them." "How do you do that?" I asked. "With a price sticker gun," he replied.

Disgusted that no one had mentioned the silly details to me, I requested a gun. Wishing it had been a real gun which I could have used about then, I started deconstructing my statuesque work of art while casting a jaundiced eye about the area and wondering when Mr. Hoyt was going to show up and fire me. I finally finished the task with my job still intact.

Soon I was up front at the checkout stands with my new, custom fitted, one-size-fits-all apron learning how to bag groceries. Being a novice, I supposed that we just threw them in the bag, but to the contrary I had things to learn. The cans go on the bottom. Bag the cold food separately. Do not overfill the bags since the customers preferred to not have their precious merchandise tumbling onto the ground.

Our active group of bagboys, Terry Ingram, Glen Hill, Ray Floyd, Mike Bowen, Ronnie Stewart and probably others whose names I forget, had a healthy sense of humor. One Saturday a cute girl smiled and waved at Terry from across the room. Having turned around and looked for another person who merited the greeting, he said, "Who? Me?" cracking up the group with guffaws.

When the store displayed a huge mock Coke roughly eight feet tall near the checkout stands to highlight the product, Ronnie Stewart in his halting Southern drawl said, "I think I will buy that thing and drink it." To understand the humor, a person had to be acquainted with Ronnie and be there to share the laughter that followed.

For an unknown reason, I escaped the joke of being sent down the street to borrow a set of "shelf stretchers." Many others before me had the joke played on them. With a new bagboy walking up to a store manager and asking him to borrow nonexistent "shelf stretchers," both involved were tested. Whatever response the store manager gave, the new bagboy always came back empty handed with an "I've-been-had" look.

Mr. Hoyt provided a one hour lunch, so some Saturdays Terry would ask Brewton Kelly, the meat department manager, to cut us slices of bologna with us adding a loaf of bread, potato chips, a jar of mayo and a Coke. Then we headed to the city park for alfresco dining. If only we had turnip greens and mayhaw jelly, we could have had a well-balanced meal.

With a quarter being big money to us, a total of eight-ten customers gave twenty-five cent tips when we carried the groceries to their cars; consequently, the bagboys learned them which created constant jockeying for position to take out their groceries.

One Saturday morning Mr. Hoyt called all the bagboys to an office in the back to hold a somber meeting, the first such encounter I had attended. He said, "You know boys when you look at those dollars in that cash register up front, you cannot tell which ones are white dollars and which ones are not." Apparently, a bagboy had committed an unacceptable act or said insulting words to a black customer which Mr. Hoyt did not receive well. He asked us to treat everyone the same which I found to be an acceptable request.

Having made a strong impression on my sense of fairness, the meeting stayed with me for fifty-two years. I could not imagine who had done that, but assuredly Mr. Hoyt had heard or seen something inappropriate. Not once did I witness Mr. Hoyt, a well-balanced manager, lose his cool of which I took note and strived to replicate in the business world.

That evening we all anticipated the clock striking 9:00 p.m. when we began to spread the red "floor-sweep" compound down the aisles and grab the big push brooms, the finishing tasks of a long day.

By 9:30 p.m. the heavily guarded Brinks armored truck had driven up with our wages in huge canvas bags. The bagboys received six dollars and thirty-nine cents for the day, a sum leaving me wondering what mathematical equation Mr. Hoyt cranked through to arrive at that number. Probably it had a proprietary origin and historians had locked it away in the National Archives for future generations to pore over.

With the money plus tips in our jeans, the group hurried out the front door acting like we were in "Fat City." I eagerly anticipated a visit to Ed's pool room and putting the largesse at risk. Later in life I proudly sprouted a brain.

Being on my feet from 6:30 a.m. in the morning until midnight gave me severe leg cramps on Saturday nights with both legs spasming and hurting badly. The price of earning and risking the big bucks did not come cheaply.

My Piggly Wiggly career came to a halt around the end of May due to Terry and me moving to Tallahassee to work at my uncle's service stations for the summer at no greater pay than Mr. Hoyt offered. Working our way up life's financial ladder, we slipped on several rungs along the way but eventually we both arrived near the top.

The time at the Piggly Wiggly left an impression on me, or I could not have recalled it so vividly after all these years. Thanks to Mr. Hoyt and Mrs. Eddie Newberry. God rest the souls of those extraordinary people.

CHAPTER 34

OFFENSES BACK TO BACK

At five o'clock on Friday afternoon in September, I hit the door of the FBI Office and headed for the old helipad down the street where the less financially endowed parked their cars. The parking beneath the building was not an alternative since it would have sucked up a major hunk of my meager pay.

Having started to work there in April of 1964, I wondered how much longer the country boy at age nineteen could handle the big city. Solicited by an FBI agent who drove up to our house one afternoon, I was flattered by the high school principal's recommendation but naïve as to the commitment I could be making. Giving me a starting point in life, the job sounded promising, but a young man that age may or may not know what he wants.

Working in the files was a boring job, a million miles away from that habitat in which I was raised. The most exciting thing that happened was the receptionist accidentally bumping the panic alarm causing a torrent of agents to storm into her office with pistols drawn. The carpet beneath her chair required detailed maintenance after each incursion.

Wheeling through the Atlanta traffic in my 1960 model Ford, South Georgia drew me with irresistible force. Going home about every weekend kept me in financial straits which reveals how I handled priorities at that age. Outside Atlanta I caught U.S. 41 which would take me the major portion of the trip home.

As most teenagers, I constantly tried to strike that balance between speed and law enforcement. For five months lending comfort to my goal of no tickets, the long arm of the law had left me alone on these trips.

When I was leaving Gay, Georgia, and drove up behind a slow-moving vehicle, my judgment went out the window as I slipped into the left lane with a state employee having painted double yellow lines at that location. My mission to go home had overridden my brain which suggested that I could be making a shaky decision. Yes, coming straight at me was a highway patrol car whose occupants had found a reason to crank up that flashing light and to release the mournful sound of their siren.

Pulling over as any law-abiding citizen, I waited for the unpleasant news resting assured that this was not a simple solicitation for the Peace Officers' Association. Offering the usual inquiry, "Didn't you see those yellow lines?" I only shook my head to squelch the opening of my mouth and avoid plowing a deeper furrow. He said he would have to radio the county Sheriff's Department to send someone out to collect a fine.

A sheriff's deputy appeared minutes afterward down the road where we met him. Happily declaring that I had a twenty-five dollar fine to cough up, he leaned against his car while I wrote a check. With his polite suggestion that I travel down U.S. 41 safely, I returned to my vehicle and continued on my trip, tugging at the wad in my shorts and trying to get some relief.

Acid ate at my stomach lining as I reviewed the events of recent minutes and made peace with my shrinking bank account. The twenty-five dollars, when accounting for inflation, would be equivalent to above two hundred dollars in today's money. Rationalizing that I would just put it behind me, take my licks and better observe the traffic laws, I pushed on with the trip.

The trooper car continued to follow me south on U.S. 41, so I tried desperately to maintain excellent driving decorum to avoid dealing with those guys again. They drifted farther and farther behind, and a light rain started falling. About five miles down the road from where I wrote the check, I came up behind a slow-moving vehicle. After following it for a distance and checking for double center lines, I pulled out for a routine pass.

The forces of fate ply their trade in dumps, if you will, leaving the unlucky under a pile, feeling dumped on, thus the expression. As the front of my car came adjacent to the left rear fender of the other car, the driver proceeded to take a left turn without a hand signal nor a turn signal being applied for the distance recommended by law. With no time for reaction, my car contacted his in the left front door, the momentum of the cars taking us off the road to the left. With the sounds of brakes applied and scraping metal, his car advanced slightly in front of mine and came to rest in a growth of hedges. I had been dumped on again in a big way. Another of life's thistles had pricked me hard.

The cushioning and slowing effect of hedges would normally be a welcome occurrence. The unsettling reality of a natural gas main in the center of the greenery caused distress. Hearing the hissing of the gas, the occupants had exited the vehicle in seconds, running a distance and stopping. Watching their actions, I assumed there must be a threat.

Guess who drives up seconds afterward? The same two troopers I had entertained down the road minutes ago. Hearing the hissing gas and having dealt with these incidents before, they ordered us to move up the road and away from the wreck. One trooper commented that we were lucky the vehicle which struck the main had stalled, or we could have been in the center of an explosion and fire. That bit of information shook my nerves.

A trooper requested my driver license. I asked if he did not still have the numbers from a few minutes ago. Stupid question. "Son, you might not get the license back this time," he snarled. Now, he had my attention as I fumbled it out of my billfold.

A fire truck showed up to secure the gas line along with that deputy sheriff I had gotten to know already. After struggling with bending my fender away from my front tire so I could drive on home, I wrote another twenty-five dollar check. In absence of the usual speeding violation, the troopers chose to charge me with "too fast for conditions" since they judged I did not properly account for the rain and adjust my speed. No mention was made of the lack of a traffic signal by the other driver. Thankfully, they returned my license.

Again wondering what could happen next, I headed the Ford south but at a controlled pace. The fender scraped when I made a right turn, but luckily I had few turns the rest of the way home.

In the mailbox about a month later, a letter from the State of Georgia arrived. It stated that my driving privileges had been revoked for a period of one year. What terrible news! How could I function without driving a car for such a long period? How could I keep my job in Atlanta? Unable to propose a better alternative, my solution was to keep driving, but carefully. Young people do not spend a lot of time languishing over decisions.

Moving back in with Mama and Daddy several months later, I felt secure that if I received a ticket for license suspension in my home county, I could handle it easier — but the saga continued.

On a Saturday night months later, I was headed down the road to our house and saw the familiar flashing lights in my mirror. Only two miles from the house, I could not believe this was happening to me. The state trooper asked for my license which I was unable to produce. Instead I offered the age-old explanations that I had lost it or it had blown away in a tornado, whichever he would prefer to believe. He wrote the ticket only for driving without an operator's license and instructed me to go to the courthouse in Bainbridge to resolve it.

After ending up on the bottom side of the dump pile so many times, life finally tossed me a cupcake. My thinking said to stay clear of the courthouse and see what would happen. After the one year suspension had ended, I received my driver license back in the mail. Never did I hear from the authorities about the ticket which needed attention in Bainbridge. The sloppiness of the criminal justice system of that era gave me a much needed break, or trooper C. A. Floyd had mercy on me and tossed the citation in the trash.

CHAPTER 35

THE MOST LOVED

On September 3, 1968, at 2:00 a.m., an Atlanta policeman rapped on the door and stated, "I am sorry to inform you. Your mother has passed away." We had no phone; therefore, my sister had called the Police Department and requested that an officer notify me. A scarcity of money in my college days had placed a limitation on communication. In shock, numb and reeling from the news, I went back into our apartment, told my wife and started preparations to travel home.

No script exists for how to behave when a loved one is lost. This was not just a loved one; this was Mama, the most-loved one I had known to that point in life. Only the heart can determine how to react based on past experiences, the closeness and the reverence the deceased invokes in the mind.

In silence we packed clothes and headed out the door. Requiring "settling-in time" to digest this tragedy of my life and move beyond denial and other heart-controlled sentiments, I headed home in a thoughtful mood. The ride home became a looped video of the times Mama and I had shared with me focusing on the laughs and the good times. She possessed a lively sense of humor which she had passed to me; I would miss that smile and the cackle.

Only a few weeks before, the last time I had seen her as I walked away from the garage door she called me back and gave me a kiss on the lips which she had never done. This gesture of love now haunted me because she had apparently sensed the finality of her life and was saying goodbye, a tenderness which had gone right over my head. Her sixty years on this earth was not enough for me, being only twenty-three years of age nor would one hundred sixty have been.

In 1946 after the birth of twins, who had survived only minutes, the doctor had recommended a complete hysterectomy for her because of an unknown health reason. Having faith that Dr. Baxley used the best judgment of the times to preserve Mama's life and health, I could not second-guess his decision. But I recognized that her health deteriorated from that point with her gaining weight and developing high blood pressure.

Never was I to have a mother who would be the picture of health and not threatened by heart disease and the ills associated. The blood pressure medication could not consistently control her hypertension and resulted in a continuing problem of bringing down the pressure surges from high levels. Periodically, she would enter the hospital for a few days to gain control of her pressure with bed rest being the chief intervention. With it going as high as 220 and me having a limited understanding of medical science, I could not understand the severity nor the associated internal damage that transpired.

In 1965 I recall her using walking therapy per the doctor's recommendation and seeing her along the highway as I returned from taking Daddy lunch where he worked at Dick Frazier's store. Watching for me coming, she had flashed the smile which could melt butter in the next room and waved me down. I knew that the walking was healthy for her, but there was no way I could not give Mama a lift. After climbing into the pickup and laughing as usual, she gave an impression that this life of ours would last forever. But we both knew better.

When we arrived at my in-law's house, I went to the bedroom to lie down sensing that the full load of her death would be bringing severe emotional pain. With the settling-in period having passed, the tears flowed in torrents as I revisited the loss and what it meant to me. The sadness of never again seeing her alive bore heavily on my mind. Realizing that I had been a loving, respectful son who appreciated her presence in my life, I was guilt-free and without any significant regrets regarding our relationship. Disappointed of her living only four years in a comfortable home which she had deserved her entire life, I perceived that life and Daddy had cheated her.

The numbers of friends and relatives who visited the house to pay respects mirrored the value of Mama to the community. Cars filled up the yard and parked on the shoulder for a distance down the road with occupants walking, sweating and fighting the gnats in the September heat as they made their way to the house. The cold death mask placed on her by the cessation of life I found difficult to accept. When I looked at her, I tried to imagine the warm, laughing, loving mother she had been.

Casey Houston, her pastor of about eight years' service, preached the funeral, but my heartache from Mama's loss blocked out his generous words. Sitting there sobbing in grief, I recalled that his predecessor Rufus Blachshear had leaned Mama back into the waters of Rock Pond after brushing back the naturally occurring, floating debris to clear a space for the immersion. The baptism had produced a glow within and outside of Mama that lasted for the rest of her life. The congregation sang her favorite song, "Amazing Grace," which expressed Mama's love of God, the Master of her heavenly reward.

Remembering those days with Mama on Sundays of my childhood, the sincere love that existed among the church's members, the lunches on the grounds and the longevity of it all, I felt pleased to have a mother who had been a part of that old institution.

With forty-six years having passed since the loss of Mama, I submit that an offspring never fully recovers from the loss of a kind and loving mother. Learning to find peace with the loss is the only sanctuary. As a cousin of mine remarked on the passing of his mama, "How do you get over losing your mama?" The simple response I would offer is, "You don't and you shouldn't. Those lingering feelings of loss are the worthwhile price of giving love and being loved."

CHAPTER 36

RAMBLED WRECK

September 1966 as I stood in a long line with hundreds of other students waiting to register for classes at Georgia Tech, I had one of those "only-in-America moments." Only three years before, I had been living in a sharecropper house and taking my daily constitutionals in an outhouse. Now I had an opportunity to pursue a degree in a fine technical school and move this Mills to a new status in life.

The one class I feared greatest at Tech was the swimming course and its rumored requirement that its graduates swim the length of the pool with their hands and feet tied together. Furthermore, as I had heard it, if anyone had to be revived they received an A in the course. If the info was only semi-factual, I still wanted no part of that course. Being a transfer-in, I was able to miss the joy of that challenge. When I swam, I wanted my limbs free and had no interest in an A for being revived. I thought revivals were best as church functions anyway.

Since I was married and living off campus, I avoided those atrocious rat hats. Talking about an uncomplimentary headdress, the beanies took the prize. The frat boys could carry that mantle.

Attending Tech home football games was the best fringe benefit of being a student. Watching Bobby Dodd on the sidelines directing his platoon of Industrial Management majors, in his always cool and business-like manner, lit my fire. The University of Georgia had its Physical Education majors so Dodd had to have a way of fielding a team with some players that were not exactly the brightest. In defense of Tech, IM was not a degree earned by riding through the campus with your car window down as PE majors were known to do. Effort had to be applied or a capable tutor, paid for by the athletic department, had to pull the jock across the finish line.

At the ball games when an attractive girl with a fine physique walked in front of the rat pool, she could expect them to rise up and chant, "Damn good box! Damn good box!" The reactions on the girls' faces had my attention. Some took the chant as flattering and basked in the glory. Others attempted to ignore the aggravators and pretend that they had no clue of why they were chanting or about what they were chanting. And then there were those who stuck their noses higher in the air and walked faster. They should have known that if their butts had not been sticking out as far as their noses were sticking up, there would have been dead quiet.

After several days at Tech, I chose to pass through the Varsity for a hamburger. The sight of the crusty old guy in the apron standing behind the counter and yelling, "Run the beef," over and over as scores of hamburgers and hot dogs came floating down a conveyor will stick in my brain forever. Yes, they had mastered volume production of junk food.

Tech students stayed in fine physical shape since the campus was in an area of high hills by this flatlander's judgment. Why they did not build the campus on a flat plain than among those knolls I will never understand. If a student were late for class and had to run up hill, he paid for it. Early on I figured out that being to class comfortably on time saved heavy sweat.

Having had no mentors or inside information of what to expect in my classes, I walked into surprise after surprise. It did not take long to discover that a portion of my colleagues took classes in secondary school that had not been dreamed of at Seminole County High School. They had intro to calculus and engineering drawing in their school curriculums. The field was not level, so I had to work that much harder.

Having not afforded a slide rule in high school, I bought one since that seemed to be standard equipment. Soon I decided that slide rules were not complimentary to my personality. Somehow I did not feel I was cyphering unless I had a pencil in my hand. To use slide rules, I needed to have grown up with them in high school. I just did not trust that sliding stick to give me the right answer. Being years ahead of hand held calculators, I was left to compute quickly and accurately by hand.

In those days females in a class were a rarity. With a limited number enrolled at the school, less than fifty percent of my classes was endowed by a member of the opposite sex. Of the ones who were in classes I attended, they added minimum sexual tension because they did not climb very high on the beauty scale. The rare, pretty ones attracted plenty of attention and had pick of the stable when it came to suitors.

The first two years were the hardest with the professors seemingly wanting to send students back home in intellectual defeat. They wanted to push me out, but I planned to stay. Being hungry for a future and certainly tired of being broke, I hung in there with a bulldog grip.

Disillusionment I must confess when it came to getting what I expected out of my education. My desire was to be given instruction that had useful applications. At no time in my career did I save the day by sitting down and cranking through a calculus algorithm. I suffered through six courses of that torture but found no use for it. Perhaps the doctoral candidates had found a practical application. Maybe they were just trying to teach me how to think. That part worked.

And then there was Rod Tappan. He was in a class with a professor that smoked but came to class without a cancer stick that day. He saw a pack in Rod's shirt pocket and asked if he could have one. Rod gave him one and he went back to the front of the class and started searching through his pockets for a light. Not finding one, he returned to Rod for a fire-up. Rod gave him some heat. After he lit it, Rod asked the professor if he should press on his chest a few times to get him started. Of course, the class broke up.

Along came the last day of class in this same tough course. The professor was talking away in front of the class when the sound of a pop top interrupts. There was Rod sucking on a beer which he toasted toward the good doctor. The professor just laughed. Rod was most different from others.

In that day a degree from Tech got a person in the building. It gave him a place to start. In no way did a new hire walk through the door knowing much. His degree just said that he had started something and finished it. Expertise had to be learned on the job, and the "final test" was yet to be taken.

In September 1970 Daddy made his only trip ever to Atlanta accompanied by Lloyd to attend my graduation. Mama had missed the date by two years and was sorely missed. For her to have been in that audience that day would have been the "crowning glory" for me, but her presence was not to be. She was there in spirit beaming from above knowing her boy had made it through college. With every reason to be proud, she must have known that she had greater influence on my cap and gown ceremony than anyone.

CHAPTER 37

NO SENSE OF HUMOR

The observant spouses among the populace identify and react to the telltale clues of a marriage irretrievably on the rocks. Friends do not need to pick up a cudgel, smack the discontented on the side of the head and yell, "It's over," loudly in their ears. The blatant signals exist in several forms: separate domiciles, separate bank accounts, loss of communication and the end of a friendship are among the high profile, easily identified hints we receive. But splitting couples must be cognizant that the other person may view the signs entirely differently and choose to react not as we assume he or she should but mad-dog crazy differently — such as my ex-spouse did.

Having thrown my valuables into the car and left a few weeks before, that big first step had been taken. Buckets of tears did not have to be emptied nor last hugs exchanged. The time was right. I knew it and she knew it. With a huge sense of relief, I drove away with scarce regrets.

A friend of mine had an affordable apartment not far from my job which worked out well. We would have our own bachelor pad with hot and cold running women parading through the joint, catering to our every whim and wish, or at least that was the brainless vision. Being free and unhampered, I could move on with my life without any serious worries, except perhaps having too much fun.

The spouse had moved on with her life. In retrospect, I realized that she had moved on with it before we separated. Human nature sometimes leads us to refuse to accept the obvious at times, so I had played my role as a card-carrying human perhaps too well and too long.

Holy hell began when I had gone back over to her apartment to retrieve an item I had missed in the flurry of the exit. Expecting to grab it and head out the door in sixty seconds, I became trapped in a conversation about us and a request that we see each other that night. Bluntly, I told her that I had plans that night and would not be available, thinking I had communicated my desire to be elsewhere effectively.

About 6:00 p.m. I picked up a young lady and headed to the Holiday Inn Airport which had a great bar that attracted a crowd. Having been upfront with her of my separated marital status, we both felt comfortable in being seen outside the shadows. Taking a seat at the crowded bar, we ordered drinks and settled down to enjoy the evening.

In 1972 Atlanta had a population above two million, with hundreds of bars available for the young to engage in the single life. There must have been fifty to seventy-five such hangouts within a short distance of my apartment. So if a person wanted to locate me that night, extensive legwork would likely be required. Wrong again, Sam.

Then I saw her walk into the busy room with a look of contempt that could change the course of a river or at least a small creek. Blinking my eyes, I took a second look. There was only one woman in Atlanta so tall, so mean and that pissed off, and she was headed in our general direction. Checking my reference frame on her and ticking off the things that could happen to us, all of which were dreadful,

I understood that my friend and I had to avoid being seen, or some-one would spend the night in the Atlanta jail, probably me and the woman scorned after the police separated us with cold water, pry bars and electric prods.

Scrooching down at the bar, miracle of all miracles, she missed us and walked into the adjoining back room which was part of the bar as well. Thinking as quickly as a quarterback with a middle linebacker on his heels, I grabbed my date's hand and led her out of the bar, fast and snappy.

Finding a restroom a distance from the bar, I gave her taxi money and told her to stay in the room for fifteen-twenty minutes and pray for her life. Heading for the stairs to the third floor which fronted on the parking lot, I posted watch on Miss Pissed-Off's car which was parked adjacent to mine. (She had surely followed me to the bar). Curiously, my army combat boots that had been left behind at her apartment had been placed on the top of my car. Thinking of the horse's head in the bed from the scene in the Godfather, I had to wonder if this was a communication of sorts. Maybe she had plans of shoving them somewhere that would cause discomfort.

Maintaining my perch, I waited for Miss Congeniality to go to her car which she did in minutes and drove away. Wiping massive beads of sweat from my forehead with a drenched, twice-wrung-out hand-kerchief, I deduced that maybe I had dodged a night in the hoosegow. The safety of my apartment sounded like a fine place to be now so I could wind down and count my blessings—another flawed decision.

As I drove into a parking place at my door, I noticed her car swerv-ing in beside mine. My luck had clearly taken a leave of absence for the evening, hopefully not my last evening. Getting out of the car, I mentally prepared for whatever battle she chose to wage on me, wishfully verbal. Unfortunately, she had left her verbal tool bag be-hind and had brought her physical tools of oppression. She came at me like a mama bear protecting her cubs, but thankfully her claws were not quite that large. Swinging at me with everything she had and some stuff she conjured up out of her not-so-balanced mind, her intentions were to inflict massive pain. Being effective on defense, I did not let her land any solid punches. Striking a "borderline lady" would be in violation of my raisin', so blocking the blows was my only alternative.

She was so mad that she became her own worst enemy. Witnessing behavior I had never before seen, I saw her become so mad that she started to collapse, ostensibly from an overload of blood pressure or hyperventilation. When she started to crumple, I would grab her to prevent an injury from her striking the pavement. When I held her vertical for a brief moment, she regained full consciousness and continued flailing away at me until she started to collapse again. After a few minutes of dancing with her in the parking lot, amidst the heads hanging out of apartment windows, I decided to move Custer's Last Stand inside my apartment.

What another dumb move! This action opened another phase of her tantrum. Now she had items to throw, of which she selected some; giving her arm a windup, she "smoked" them in my direction. Picking up my buddy's hefty glass ashtray, she performed a couple of discus thrower rotations and released the projectile which could have been clocked at above one hundred miles per hour as it narrowly spun by my head. Not only did it embed in the wallboard, but it protruded through into the adjacent apartment with me hoping no one was at home. Next she turned over our television cart and television in her guttural desire to wreak destruction of whatever and whoever she could wreak it. With us both yelling, she continued to bombard me with whatever would fit in her hand until sheer exhaustion claimed her.

Finally, she weaved her way out of my apartment, entered her car and disappeared, the best thing that had happened to me in the last hour. Having seen this woman I used to love denigrate her demeanor and my apartment and leave in such a sad, solemn way was an empty victory.

The next time I would see Sweet Thang would be in a lawyer's office which worked out well for both of us. Being my one and only divorce, I could not fathom couples going through that more than once.

I was so glad her friend did not lend that pistol she had demanded early in the evening — late-breaking news that I learned a week or so afterward.

CHAPTER 38

A HEINOUS ACT

S ometime in the late summer months of 1966, I stepped from Jerry and Chester "Suggy" Alday's car and told them, "See you later." Taking life for granted, friends easily overlook the role of providence. Yes, I would see them again if life had no other plans.

Those two straight arrows were as well-brought-up and trustworthy as any young men Seminole County had produced. Living as honest, God-fearing, hardworking, responsible, teetotalers with irreproachable integrity, they were friends to everyone that came in contact with them.

Having spent countless hours riding around the Tastee Freeze with them, shooting the breeze and looking for girls, who might look back at us, I was proud to call them friends. With as many as five in the car including them, we found entertainment by riding around and wishing that we could charm the ladies. When they needed a break from Donalsonville, we would ride over to Chandler's Hamburgers in Bainbridge. If I did not have money for a Coke, sharing what they had, they bought me one.

In September I enrolled at Georgia Tech and they went on with their farming operation. Both intent on finding that special mate, having a family and growing old together, they were married within several years.

Hearing about them next in 1973, I had recently married Connie with us living in Foster City, California, and working in San Francisco. A friend of mine from Atlanta, with whom I had worked, called and asked if I knew the Aldays. Remarking that I probably did, I realized the Aldays comprised a sizeable extended family. He read their names from a newspaper, bringing astonishment and horror simultaneously to me. Jerry, Chester, Jimmy, Ned, Ned's brother and Chester's wife Mary had been murdered. Shocking! How could this have happened in low-crime Seminole County?

A month or so later, Connie and I traveled to Atlanta and on to Donalsonville for a brief, belated honeymoon. Always having been a down-to-earth person of simple tastes, she delighted in the visit to the rural South for her first time.

Visiting the cemetery with those head stones in black granite, the starkness and harsh reality of it proved to be an awful mind-rattler. Those loved and respected individuals should not have been there. Life had dealt a severe blow to their family and to the citizens of the county who loved them.

Four escaped convicts from Maryland had found their way to Donalsonville and spotted Mary, Suggy's wife, leaving the Piggly Wiggly and following her home. The Alday men, working in the fields near the house, came to the house on tractors one at a time and were shot by the despicable pretexts for human beings. Abusing Mary, the convicts left her body in a pasture not far away.

With anger running high among their family and friends, when the prisoners had been captured, they had to be moved to another jail in Albany for their safety. The community, losing solid citizens with vast family and friend connections, was in a stir.

By no measure was justice served by bouncing the guilty around the court system for decades, avoiding resolution. Only one offender was executed, Carl Isaacs the ringleader, in 2003 after thirty years on death row. Presenting a prime opening for criminal justice reform in Georgia, the case may have brought changes in the laws, but I am unsure of whether it happened.

Today River Road where the lives were taken has the father's name Ned Alday on its road-marker sign. How appropriate! Anyone who knew them cannot read that road sign without remembering what happened and the senselessness of it. The Aldays, victims of such an unspeakably heinous act, should be held in our memories.

Today individuals habitually carry guns in the county and elsewhere in our country. The innocent need that protection against those with whom they may come in contact who could do them harm. Fate can throw the innocent into a dangerous encounter anytime and anywhere. Always carrying a weapon, I remain assured that "I would rather walk my way through court than tiptoe around self-defense," as a smart person once said.

CHAPTER 39

IN THE HANDS OF DESTINY

After arriving at the San Francisco airport, I strolled up to a counter and asked a young woman for directions to the rental car desks. Repeating my question three times before she deciphered my request, I received help. I walked away wondering whether I could not talk plain or the lady could not listen plain. Miscommunications would continue since a country boy from South Georgia with a Southern drawl had an inherent challenge getting his point across in this far away metropolis.

Taking in the stunning scenery of the bay and the downtown skyline, I drove to the Mission District for a job interview. A buddy of mine who formerly worked at Arrow Shirts in Atlanta, Georgia, had asked that I visit to determine whether there would be a fit for me in the Lilli Ann organization, a designer and manufacturer of high end ladies' coats and suits.

The interviews went well so I flew back to Atlanta to give my resignation and make plans to move to the Bay Area while divorcing my wife on the way out of town, ironically on Friday, October 13, a good omen. A clean break from the marriage and the city offered promise for a better life on the Gold Coast. Delighted that I had received a seventy-five percent increase in salary but expecting only a thirty-five to forty percent increase in the cost of living which would leave me with additional disposable income, I thought that I had cut the proverbial "fat hog."

Oblivious at the time, I had failed to recognize the defining moment of the trip which was riding speechless in a Lilli Ann building elevator with the most beautiful woman I had ever seen in person, though she was accompanied, which softened the blow of my awkwardness. The forty-five second encounter with an angel too gorgeous for me to have a conversation with or barely acknowledge hung tightly in my mind and refused to fade. Struggling to dismiss the chance encounter as a flash instant in time, I wondered what it would be like to know her, incubating a self-perpetuating fantasy.

For the bulk of the trip in October 1972, I traveled U.S. 66, the highway made famous by Martin Milner and George Maharis in the television series, "Route 66." With plentiful small town scenery along the way, I experienced a slice of Americana and its beauty. Looking back, only two memories of the trip remained clearly in my mind: Las Vegas, the loneliest city in the country when a traveler is unaccompanied, and the Mojave Desert with its flat, arid, empty, moonlike landscape and outrageously hot temperatures.

Arriving in the locality, I assumed my duties and settled in an apartment in San Mateo. Lilli Ann had a personality of its own imposed by Adolph Schuman, the eccentric owner. A canny businessman in his mid-sixties, he had built an organization producing high style women's wear the clientele loved. Older, wealthy females graded their status in life by the number of Lilli Ann's they had in their closets. With borderline gauche styling and select fashions crossing that line, Mr. Schuman had carved out a niche in the fashion business.

Referred to by the staff as "The Zoo" Lilli Ann had a unique culture of the extreme variety. Mr. Schuman's two miniature poodles, constantly chasing each other, yelping and infrequently depositing surprises for the unwary to find with their shoes, had free run of the building and the factory. Of course, they were not the only animals in The Zoo.

Adolph was not a man of patience with his total inventory of the commodity equaling zero. Having Terryphones, components of a paging system, hanging on columns in various locations throughout the complex, when a manager or designer heard their name spoken by Mr. Schuman, accompanied by the words "pick up, pick up," they raced for the nearest phone. He would state his information or command, and the recipient responded in the affirmative.

The best use of the Terryphones came on random Friday afternoons when he would summon the members of management to hang out in the conference room and enjoy drinks, a fringe benefit. Bottles of Chivas Regal scotch and wine loosened tongues and launched cheery moods, the reasonable price of listening to his tales of John Kennedy, skin diving, race horses at Deauville in France or whatever he wanted to share. After an hour or so of free drinks, we started drifting out of the conference room as he started planning dinner or other amusements with his striking girlfriend, half his age.

Having been a key supporter of John Kennedy in California during the 1960 election campaign, Adolph knew Mr. Kennedy personally and hung enlarged images of the president's doodles on the walls. Joan Kennedy visited once, and Mr. Schuman ordered his design staff to create ten ensembles with her measurements that the factory produced gratis, affording an opportunity for the management staff to witness the largesse of those associated with power.

Indeed, I experienced culture shock when holidays brought a celebration with tables abutted end to end on the factory floor at lunchtime. With the Mission District being a melting pot, we had factory personnel from the far corners of the Earth. The dishes of food the seamstresses placed on the tables took our staff on an exceptional cuisine tour of various countries. Never again have I enjoyed such a delicious variety of culinary offerings at one meal. Accompanying the food was wine and hard liquor which made me wonder of the straightness of seams sewed in the afternoon.

Since I was taken by the exaggerated anything-goes culture, I concluded that this was an exclusive society, bearing no similarities whatsoever to the South and my roots. Though a young man could warm up to it.

Lunches at Mama's, an Italian bar and restaurant, enticed our management on Fridays because she offered prawns salad, containing huge shrimp, much larger than the size I was accustomed to from Florida. With each lunch order, a patron received two, ten ounce bottles of burgundy red wine, vinted late yesterday afternoon. Customers usually left a portion of their wine and would push the bottles to the middle of the table. Therefore patrons who lingered had all the red wine they wanted to drink for as long as they cared to imbibe. Lunches became lengthy at times with my buzzed bosses not watching the clock, facilitating their making of difficult work decisions on Friday afternoons with a focus on those personnel judgments which the manager may have been delaying.

Across the street from the workplace, adjacent to railroad tracks, was the Whistle-stop Bar and Café where we conducted many informal management meetings over lunch. Serving sandwiches and red wine (Wine and a glass of water were standard fare for lunches.) with its rustic, well worn, barstool ambience, it proffered an escape from the tribulations of the job. After work, we frequently stopped in for a drink and to rehash the day's skirmishes.

Receiving an invitation to a party which included various associates, I arrived not knowing what to expect since this was my first of such affairs. With a double "lo and behold," I noticed the beautiful brunette from the elevator and treasured the thought of being in the same room and breathing the same air.

In a few minutes, after putting a couple glasses of courage under my belt which mustered up the maximum confidence that my psyche could produce, I walked up to her, formally met Connie Harman and started chatting, still sipping the valor juice. After visiting several minutes and noticing the scarcity of seating, we chose to sit on the carpeted floor to enjoy our chardonnay and continue becoming acquainted with each other for the rest of the evening.

Maintaining eye contact while savoring her splendor and Midwest charm, a rapport struck us both that was undeniable. The down-to-earth nature of this exquisite lady communicated unpretentious, sincere and genuine while oozing femininity to the ultimate. Noticing her hands, I decided they were the most beautiful I had ever seen with long slender fingers, perfect nails and flawless skin.

We easily conversed about whatever came up and started plundering in each other's heads. The evening ended with me cautiously asking her for a date with her response, to my amazement, being, "Yes."

Our first date about the first week in December was at Alioto's restaurant, adjacent to the San Francisco Wharf where we started to become friends and escalated the feel-good sense of comfort to the next level. She showed me her apartment on the twenty-third story of the Embarcadero Center which had a balcony overlooking downtown. Watching the fog roll in from the bay late at night with this fair lady far exceeded my expectations in life, a perfect venue for driving an arrow through the heart.

One of our favorite dating haunts was Ripples, located on the twenty something floor of a building in the heart of downtown San Francisco. Usually six or eight staff from Lilli Ann would accompany Connie and me to this Temple of the Gods of Booze and Fun having a personality all its own. After 5:00 p.m., the challenge of wedging through the door and into the standing-room-only crowd became the price of entry. If the city had fire codes, the clientele constantly abused them to some multiple of the extent of the law. People drank or danced, or danced while drinking to the ever-blasting latest rock. Since the waitresses had a hard time finding a patron again, the best way to get a drink was to head to the bar which had a video scene of waves crashing on a beach for the full length of the counter. Watching the scene while downing a few scotches would make a patron wonder if he were sea sick or spirits heavy.

The restrooms had uniqueness and patron practices unlike this young man had ever seen or imagined. Constantly males went into the ladies room to view the giant nude Burt Reynolds Cosmopolitan magazine neon lighted layout with his hand strategically placed to cover his fishing tackle and to eye the ladies primping at the mirrors. Likewise, the ladies would just walk into the men's room to watch the guys doing their business at the urinals while watching free shady videos on the wall. Everyone got a huge laugh and generally minded their manners with the risqué customs.

To break up the routine, the gang often visited the Royal Exchange Bar on Sacramento Street which began business the year we met and attracted business associates from the financial district including young dating couples such as us. Loads of chrome and black decorated the place with seats on the side next to the picture windows and the traffic being the most desired since the establishment was on street level. A recent search of the internet indicated that it was still there and thriving. It would be fun to go back, but we quit drinking a couple years ago so it would not be the same.

Visiting Fisherman's Wharf for cracked crab came to be one of our favorite excursions. Not being an expert on crab, I would guess that it was King Crab because the legs were the largest I had ever seen. The servers would crack the legs for the patrons so the juicy, tasty meat was easy to access in large chunks. After that experience, I have not been able to suffer through cracking and picking out the meat from the smaller Southern crabs.

During the coming days, we were inseparable spending abundant time together and enjoying each other's presence. Being close to Christmas, she told me of an annual planned trip home to visit with her family. This troubled me, her leaving for roughly a week, but understanding the commitment she had and the newness of our relationship, I could not expect to go along. Spending the loneliest

Christmas of my life, we spoke on the phone two or three times, and I hung out with my best buddy's girlfriend since he had gone home for the holidays, also.

When she returned, I silently promised to avoid the uneasy feeling of being separated again from this special woman. On Wednesday night, January 17, 1973, I casually suggested that we should marry the coming weekend in Reno. Just as nonchalantly, she answered, "Yes, we should." The unplanned nature of the conversation on my part and her off the cuff answer to the suggestion cemented a bond and a relationship. Marriage counselors would question the success of a marriage where the couple had gone together only six weeks, but we defied the experts and the odds, developing a permanent connection which would not be broken.

Connie called her mother that night sharing the happy news, and they made plans for the weekend in Reno, Nevada. Late Friday afternoon her mother, father and two sisters, Rebecca (age 25) and Mary (age 24) flew in with us meeting them at the airport. The source of Connie's looks was apparent as I observed that her mother and two sisters were strikingly beautiful as well.

Joining our celebration, my best man and his girlfriend had followed us from San Francisco, so our group dined at a restaurant in a casino and then took the party back to our rooms. Connie's family enjoyed a toast of wine or scotch so we came to know each other with hair let way down. I had a perception of fitting in with her family and thought the feelings were mutual.

Busy the next morning Connie and I had a do list: finding a wedding chapel and obtaining a marriage license. Looking through the yellow pages, I saw a multitude of offerings from wedding chapels with a variety of catchy names. Being conservative, I chose one with the humdrum name of "The Wedding Chapel," slotting a time near noon, complete with photography of our choosing.

Securing a marriage license proved to be a simple process which must have been a source of pride for the city government in view of the number of couples who came there to marry. Marching into the Reno courthouse, presenting ID's, signing forms and paying a fee took us about ten minutes.

Converging on The Wedding Chapel at the appointed time, we were married culminating what most would call a whirlwind courtship. The photographer snapped a series of photographs, treasures which would be mailed to us in a wedding book. Swapping sugar with the love of my life and confirming with "I dos," we sealed the pact which has lasted four decades plus.

Having been awarded a divorce decree in Atlanta on Friday, October 13, 1972, I had no conception that I would marry again three months hence, but that is the upside of the spontaneity of life and a notion in the heart that feelings are right with a relationship. When I consider the long odds of pulling the two of us together with a focused effort, much less finding each other accidentally, I must yield to the guidance of a power beyond us.

Our love has grown over these forty-two years with a minimum of small bumps along the way, but not any we could not willingly find a way over or through. I recall one of my brother Lloyd's favorite maxims regarding the ladies, "When you trade, be sure to trade up"—and so I did.

CHAPTER 40

THE SOUTHERN KITCHEN

W hat amount of trouble can a man encounter without trying? Until the fall of 1977, the question had never arisen for me so if asked, I could not have given a descriptive answer because previously I had solicited my own trouble on purpose. Unknowingly, that query had me in hot pursuit, hell bent on ruining a football weekend and placing me in a Class A predicament.

The year we lost Elvis placed me in Pauls Valley, Oklahoma, executing a distribution center engineering assignment for a jeans manufacturing organization. Five months into the assignment, the Division Manager informed me of their annual bus trip to Dallas for a football game, a rather mundane, uneventful affair until now. With the Cowboys and the Redskins on the card, he invited me to join the management team and some local dignitaries from towns where manufacturing facilities were located for a day of football and socializing, perhaps realistically described as boozing with sandwiched-in football. Looking back, the game went well, but the fun, as it does at times, had unknowns tucked away, including a resounding I-cannot-believe-it.

As the chartered Trailways bus bounced out of the parking lot at the office building, a six pack of quart Coca Colas tumbled from the back seat with one bottle breaking, releasing Coke syrup to flow about the bus floor randomly. Had I possessed a crystal ball, it would have been helpful to inquire of it, "Does that liquid all over the floor have a bearing on the outcome of our trip?" The upcoming understanding of the Coke syrup's contribution gave me awe-inspiring pause.

With thirty-five to forty partiers on the bus, along with the unbroken Cokes and a river of spirits and beer, the fun gun was locked and loaded. Partying all the way to the game, during the game and on the bus back home seemed the only way to maximize our enjoyment of the day. A planned stop for dinner after the game at a well-known Dallas landmark, The Southern Kitchen, would cap off the trip and was anticipated by everyone, being an opening to dilute the booze with food and begin that slow climb up the sobriety ladder.

Cruising down the road in comfort, we all partook of the drinks, visited loudly and enjoyed the ride as the Coke syrup, meandering about the bus, mingled with the dirt on the floor fashioning a sweet, slick mud. With every additional drink, the footing became less stable.

With the bus lurching as I walked down the aisle, guess what happened to Sam? He slipped and fell to the floor on his butt in an ungentlemanly manner. The Coke on the floor had taken its toll. As I sat there for a moment and laughed, a fellow partier whom I did not know tipped his beer on top of my head. Struggling to take this wanton act in stride, I returned to my feet and stated, "It's a good thing that I have a good nature, or we would fight." Smiling at him and thinking nothing of the slight dousing, I weaved my way back to my seat to mix another joy juice.

Arriving at the Cowboy stadium, our group was mellow and ready for some football. With seats together in the same section, the atmosphere of celebration continued as we settled in for the game. My fuzzy recollection says that the Dallas team won, but after these many years and that much alcohol being consumed that day, I cannot be sure.

Filing back on the bus, we all anticipated dinner at the Southern Kitchen where we arrived in minutes. With the seating desk positioned a distance from the door, we formed a long line inside the building and awaited tables.

While standing there patiently, the man in front of me in line, in a flash, took a straight-on jab at my head with his right fist. Seeing it coming, I barely had time to lean my face away from the punch with it burning the side of my face. Recovering, as he pulled his arm and fist back, I yelled, "Is he fooling?" but the look in his eyes had already answered that question. My emotions and defense hormones started doing my thinking for me, driving me to hit him with every fist I had and to wish that additional ones had been available. Somehow, we ended up on the floor still swinging and tangled up like two rabid dogs.

My friends separated us which could have prevented abuse, especially of me, but it had risks attached for the Samaritans. Monday morning the Division Engineer sported a swollen jaw which he said came from one of my errant fists, the one with my college class ring on a finger.

Successfully pulling us apart, they wanted to put distance between us because I was a mad Irishman who had been sucker-punched with no conception of why it had happened. Little ol' one hundred seventy-five pound me wanted to dismember this forty-something year old, two hundred fifty pound banker from Idabel, Oklahoma, who had been a lineman on the Oklahoma State football team in his college days. Soaking him with every oath and curse word in my vocabulary plus a few I extemporaneously contrived on the spot, I tried to communicate to him how pissed off I was.

The Southern Kitchen would do without our business that night, effectively throwing our group out of the restaurant. When we returned to the bus, my friends ushered me to the back seat, and his friends accompanied him on the front seat.

Strapping him to the hood of the bus would have been a wiser decision since the visual of him provoked my continuing verbal bouquets to be tossed in his direction. If I had to choose a moment in my life and declare it to be my maddest, this provocation would be the uncontested choice. Without known justification, a stranger had taken a swing at me which would have taken out all my front teeth if he had connected. The low-down move had unraveled me like nothing else in my thirty-two years. Besides that, the alcohol in my system threw fuel on the fire, elevating my temper to an even higher crescendo.

The management team, without that scrumptious dinner we all had counted on, carried unspoken animosity for me and my fighting buddy. The now quiet group rode back to Pauls Valley wondering what had happened as I did.

Along the way, the Division Manager had heated words with the gentleman from Idabel and threatened to throw him off the bus.

What a mess! I asked again, "How does an easy going redneck from South Georgia find turmoil by minding his own business?"

With me still suffering from the unanswered question of why this happened, Monday morning a friend of mine on the management team came to me.

He said, "Remember your fall on the bus on the way to the game?"

Saying, "Yes," I could not imagine what that had to do with anything. His next statement was the kicker.

He explained, "I saw the guy dump the beer on your head so for revenge I dumped part of my drink in the seat of his pants."

Now a fuzzy image of what transpired started to take shape. When I fell, the aisle was crowded with people standing nearby. In that pile of humanity, my friend had wet the back of the man's pants, and the man from Idabel had concluded that I had done it. How twisted can assumptions and the facts become?

The Division Manager had spoken to my boss and explained what really happened so my job nor reputation was jeopardized by the unbelievable events of the weekend. I counted my blessings to have the quick reaction time to avoid that punch and the ability to mount a defense against an unexpected act of attempted violence. In that frantic tussle at the Southern Kitchen, the big fellow from Idabel had not laid a fist on me. I had bounced some licks off him but had walked away unhurt knowing that with his size if he had gotten a solid punch, the damage could have been traumatic, a possible consequence requiring new teeth for me and a visit to a plastic surgeon.

CHAPTER 41

GUN/FIGHT AT PRYOR'S CORRAL

I n the '60s and '70s, Pryor Lane's liquor store and bar was the choice for resident imbibers. Pryor's resume included being a life-long citizen of the county with deep family roots and service in The Big War which brought undying reverence from the locals who knew him.

The business, located at Hagan's Still crossing between the railroad tracks and US 84, a comfy, cozy place for his patrons, had furnishings of five or six bar stools, a table and chairs for dominos, a bar and Pryor. Pryor, not a long winded individual but when he spoke, he had something real to say. Patrons could not help but love the guy with his being sincere, genuine, down-to-earth and honest. The welcome mat always was out for me and my brothers since we were relatives as well as friends.

Laughs, wild tales and an abundance of "Lord Calvert sandwiches" friends shared freely (The Lord Calvert being sandwiched between the ice cubes). The latest man gossip flowed as liberally as the Lord Calvert, leaving the listeners to sort fact from fiction; embellishments were rampant.

Circa 1968 my brother Lloyd and his friend Larry Batchelor operated Hill Pace's former service station in Iron City. Home from college for a summer weekend, I stopped in late in the afternoon to visit, soon hearing a suggestion that we go to Ed's pool room after they closed the station. With all three of us being pool lovers, we had quick concurrence.

Larry left first, planning to stop at Pryor's for a quick drink to "settle his nerves" for the upcoming games. Lloyd and I left in my car and, of course, Lloyd wanted to stop at Pryor's as well and agreed that after a drink or two we would proceed on to the billiard parlor.

We parked the car and walked toward the entrance and as we reached the door, Larry came backing out with a gentleman, a relative of ours, following him and pointing a pistol at Larry's midsection. To preserve peace in the family, I will not mention his name.

My brain started racing and running down a checklist of historical references. Had I ever witnessed a person pointing a gun at another? No. Had I ever seen such a serious look on a face as the one with the gun? No. A check of my archives indicated scenes of this content only happened in the movies, or exceptional true life events. Noticing the absence of a camera and crew, I had to deal with the crisis.

Lloyd with his hair trigger temper said to me, "I'm going to the car and get my shotgun." He and Larry had been close friends since high school, so at my first consideration, I extrapolated that act had to be a no-go possibility. One gun indicated a man could maybe be shot. A second gun involved greatly increased the probability of blood spilling on the ground outside of Pryor's. Having earned an A in probability at Georgia Tech, I was closely in touch with the chances so an intervention seemed appropriate.

I outran Lloyd to the car and grabbed the gun, preventing his futile attempt to take it away. My brother going to jail for shooting a guy trying to shoot another guy would not happen that day. Besides the justice system could make one of its famous errors as it had done previously.

Meanwhile Larry and the gentleman, addressing each other with harsh words not found in any Sunday school lesson plan, raised the conflict to another level at least by a decibels measure. Then, with a lightening flash from his right arm, Larry connected with a right which sent the gun spinning into the shrubbery. Yes, Pryor's had shrubs, one of its many standout, homey features.

Next, we all relished in the joy of the man's son driving up in a pickup, bolting out with a claw hammer, taking this scrape to another level of danger. Larry, being a fighter that was way better than average with his fists, dispatched with the son as well, avoiding spilling blood on the hammer.

By then, the fight had dwindled to cussing and fussing with the gentleman searching the shrubs for his gun and Larry checking the wear and tear on his knuckles. Knowing that Pryor had called the sheriff, I told Lloyd the time was right for us to exit after tempting fate sufficiently on this hot summer evening.

Later that night Larry said that the man persisted in searching for the gun when the sheriff's deputy arrived. Believing the usual story of the good old boys having a mild disagreement, the officer kept the scrapers out of jail. No harm came to anyone other than a sore jaw or two with not a drop of blood hitting the ground.

When asking Larry why there was such a high level of animosity, he said, "It involved trapping quail." Larry would trap quail since that eliminated any need to pick birdshot out of them as we all were familiar. This technique, being somewhat outside the game laws, and an ongoing hatred between them set the stage for the gentleman to report Larry to the game wardens who seized his traps. That day at Pryor's, Larry had commented to the gentleman about the game wardens and escalation followed. Out came the gun, an act causing all the excitement to "hit the fan."

Lloyd thanked me the next morning for not letting him have the gun. With a cooler head, he realized that I was just keeping him clear of possible trouble.

CHAPTER 42

A GOOD WHUPPIN'

A portion of the following story was told me by my nephew Ben Sketo who was twelve years my junior. He conveyed it two-three years after the incident over a bottle of Jack and Coke while we sat in easy chairs by our swimming pool. His version included the right balance of embellishments and truths which expressed his own uniqueness. Perhaps I can partially recapture that notorious day he described. This narrative is dedicated to his memory since Ben passed in 1987 at age thirty from kidney disease complications.

Circa 1979 Larry Batchelor owned a bar and liquor store in Iron City which thrived in its heyday being a favorite respite for its loyal patrons. The joint had two or three pool tables and a dominos table which attracted customers who could understand simple mathematics. Not everyone played, obviously. Next door, under the same roof, resided his package store which under Georgia law required a separate room and entrance. Completing the décor was a long bar with eight or ten bar stools.

Drawing rednecks like a free-beer barbecue, the establishment was a beehive of activity. Many of them coming to visit with the

Lord — "Lord Calvert." Not that I carried a card declaring "I am a redneck," but I liked the place. Larry's father Collie helped behind the bar, and Larry bought gold from anyone who had a need for money greater than the gold, always offering a semi-fair price to the seller and a fair price to Larry.

Our nephew Ben Sketo at ages twenty-two to twenty six spent significant time with Uncle Lloyd, staying with him in a mobile home outside of Iron City. Living in Tallahassee with his mother, Ben loved the adventure of being with his Uncle Lloyd which drew him to Iron City, frequently. Hunting, fishing and hanging around with wild fellows appealed to his personality. Fitting in well, Ben experienced tough lessons of life and added select tricks to his repertoire that he would have been better off missing.

One afternoon Ben occupied his favorite barstool at Larry's with Lloyd and his ever- present friend B.O. Batchelor. B.O. served as a cook in the Army Special Forces before retiring years back. What a guy! Sapping every second of life out of every day, he had lost his last tooth recently and possessed no inclination to get dentures for the moment. He did not hold teeth in a priority status, but drinking, boozing and carousing had an honored position at the top of his list.

He was famous locally for grabbing a lizard from a wall during a card game, gumming it to death and swallowing it, a feat which he had learned in Special Forces training. Some "hoity toity" poker players became nauseated with the lizard's tail wiggling out of B.O.'s mouth and left the game early.

If a person grew up around Iron City in the '50s, he knew of Thomas Story. Thomas, six-eight years older than me and totally absent of socially-redeeming qualities, carried a black cloud everywhere he went. A derelict in school, he had changed not one iota after leaving the institution. Disappearing for a long period, Thomas had returned to Iron City in recent years.

Thomas walked into the bar that afternoon, circa 1980, looking for trouble and he found it. Lloyd and B.O. sat on bar stools with Ben, and Collie bartended as Thomas walked up to the bar. A weighty fellow, over six feet and well above two hundred pounds, Thomas pushed B.O. from his bar stool onto the floor, unprovoked. Then the fracas began as Lloyd and B.O. started pummeling him from all directions, and Thomas began to understand that he had stirred up an octopus with fourteen arms and fists. Stretching him out on a pool table, Lloyd and B.O. maintained their assault with Thomas beyond resistance. Minutes afterward, trying to recover from a beat-down fog, he rose up on one elbow and said, "Boys, I was just kiddin'."

Ben could strum on his guitar, so several years later he and I in a happy mood by our pool near Murfreesboro, Tennessee, decided to write a song about the fight entitled "Just Kiddin'." The handwritten page containing the words disappeared over the years, but I remember the chorus: "Just kiddin', just kiddin'. The good ol' boy was just kiddin'. What you have to know about good ol' boys is when they are just kiddin'." The full song captured the spirit of the fight, in all of its hilarity. Our one chance at Nashville fame and I had lost the words.

Circa 1982 I saw Larry outside the bar as Lloyd and I were leaving, noticing his weak handshake from the toll of cirrhosis and alcohol. The sincere sign of affection persisted with the lighting up of his eyes, but his flame was headed for burn-out at age forty-seven. Thanks for the memories, Larry. Rest in peace.

CHAPTER 43

THE WOLF AT BAY

Looking for a job in May 1971 was not the essence of timing. With a recession in process, it had the characteristics of being the worst job market in years. Businesses had shied away from Georgia Tech as a politician shies from the truth. I had chalked up only one interview with a pipeline company which produced no offer. Feeling rejected and dejected, I fell out of love with me and my desperate situation.

Desiring to stay in Atlanta, I contacted headhunters for help in finding a job, hopefully a position in a solid national company. Receiving an interview with Arrow Shirts and being interviewed by a Southern Tech graduate, an embarrassment of proportions, I secured a placement at their East Point, Georgia, facility as plant engineer. A career in the apparel business had never entered my mind, but when a man needs a job, he broadens his horizons.

An industrial engineer applies his skills to improving processes, possessing an understanding that processes can always be more efficient through technical analysis and subsequent changes. Perfect processes do not exist since improved methods of achieving a result, an output in process lingo, can always be found. Continuous improvement which creates more value for the customers and additional profit for the company is always the objective.

From the beginning, my coerced affection of the sewing industry brought plentiful question marks. The labor intensive nature of the work and the dinosaur state of processes dampened my spirits since I had pictured working in a sophisticated industry with generous budgets which funded technology-oriented process improvements. This industry lay at the bottom of the pile of my perceived sought-after work environments.

Being a closet perfectionist, my toleration of how the plant operated and its narrow- minded management created internal conflict. In about a year, I was promoted to the job of chief engineer which brought a modicum of solace for my ambition.

A novice in business, I did not understand that when a person works in an industry, there lies a point beyond which the strain of moving to another industry, with starting at the bottom again and the associated pay cut, outweighs job dissatisfaction. Eventually, a few years later the reality hit me; I was stuck.

Geography was never a limitation as I moved to better jobs with higher pay but finding the same old backward industry. In retrospect, a job counselor would have cautioned that the best thing for me was to settle down with one of these organizations and live with whatever bothered me. I had spent too much time in that place called "in retrospect." Being my own personnel counselor, I chose to sort it out alone with my best judgment and proceed as a half-happy employee. I quit looking back.

My wife and I had the vagabond experience of living in nine states: Tennessee, Alabama, Mississippi, California, Colorado, Texas, Louisiana, South Dakota and Georgia. Counting up the number of times we moved in my career yielded a total of fifteen, a portion due to moving into temporary living space while finding a home to buy in a given locale, and some relocations accommodated intercompany transfers. Since a preponderance of moving company stickers decorated the underside of our furniture, we were reminded of our frequent moves over and over. Moving had at least one advantage of throwing away junk each time we relocated preventing any need to ever rent temporary storage space.

On my favorite two jobs, I worked as an internal consultant who analyzed and improved operations with one objective, reducing costs. Catching a plane on Mondays and returning on Fridays for ten years bothered me terribly leaving Connie alone and having a life on the phone four nights a week, but I gained valuable knowledge in process improvement. Living well and recognizing we had to play the only game in town, we made the best of the undesirable circumstances.

As we ripped pages off the calendars, I noticed that the apparel industry had begun an accelerating trend of moving overseas. The fifty cents per hour labor in Asian countries attracted labor-intensive garment production. Comparably, the United States' cost of about eight dollars per hour was uncompetitive in global markets for apparel, a reality resulting in the clothing industry having no choice but to chase the cheap labor. A dwindling supply of American jobs bothered me since I had no desire in the latter portion of my career to travel the world and handle the complications associated, mainly extensive time away from Connie.

Being frugal, we had always saved money from the time we were first married. Investing in mutual funds over the years, we had accumulated a nest egg.

During the mid-nineties, when I was plant manager of an operation in Athens, Texas, which manufactured cheerleader uniforms, I began dabbling with investments in stocks of companies, a new challenge versus mutual funds — and riskier. After spending time learning the ropes, cutting my teeth and losing some of them, I became aggressive as the internet investment craze bloomed. Slowly in '96, '97, I gained knowledge and bet larger sums of money recognizing that the market had tremendous possibilities for growth of capital.

Two events produced the path for me to retire in 1998: first, I owned a sizeable portion of the "house's" money and second I virtually hated the job I had as operations manager for a cheerleader organization in Memphis, Tennessee. Hired under false pretenses which made me irate, I sought a way out. Not knowing it at the time, I had a job which had produced a strong motivation within me. The circumstances caused me, cognizant that domestic jobs in my industry were becoming scarce, to focus on my portfolio to find a financial way out of the company and out of my work life. In July 1998 I had sufficient money to walk away, an unbelievable accomplishment and an exhilarating feeling of freedom.

We spent another year in Memphis where I applied my energies to the stock market and my portfolio grew larger.

Feeling comfortable in leaving Memphis, we moved in May 1999 to Lynn Haven, Florida, an area Connie and I had always liked. The beauty and allure of Panama City, Florida, and the surrounding communities hooked its claws into us with a no-give grasp. Proximity to Seminole County, Georgia, and my home town supported the choice.

Continuing to be full invested in the market, my portfolio blossomed beyond my wildest dreams. Then, Fed Chairman Greenspan determined that he had to kill the investment bubble by raising interest rates. Having watched my investments peak and valley over five years, I hesitated with acknowledging his willed destiny for the market which would destroy stock values.

What happens with a person who has seen substantial success in the markets is the loss of appreciation for the value of money. The dollars had become a means of keeping score rather than the security which could guarantee our futures in a grand fashion. Feelings of all-knowing and all-powerful briefly found their way into my psyche, to my chagrin.

My investments peaked in value in March of 2000 at a level I could never have dreamed. Watching a portion of my portfolio disappear and reappear so often in the past, I expected the market to turn up again. Between March 2000 and December of that year, I saw enough money disappear to retire two or three additional times, but I had chosen a point at which I would sell to preserve a comfortable retirement.

One afternoon in December 2000 while noticeably shaking with the anxiety of a man tied to railroad tracks and a train bearing down, I moved my assets to cash which was hard to do because that action cemented the loss of the "house money" I would have kept had I not been greedy and had sold shares earlier. A tremendous lesson I learned too late for it to matter.

Later that month I committed the money to conservative management by a well-known investment company, acknowledging that if I kept my fingers in that pie, there could be a sad ending to our story. I walked away with ten times the initial investment and did not look back while thanking the Good Lord for blessing us so generously.

Next to marrying Connie, retiring at age fifty-two was the best thing that had happened to me. To wake up in the morning with obligations to no one but my family was extraordinarily satisfying. Those people who retire and regret it out of boredom have a lack of imagination. Our lives were as full as we wanted them to be.

We had a lovely, spacious home bayside in the Panama Country Club with abundant friends and activities constantly on the agenda. The immaculately landscaped neighborhood with a golf course, clubhouse and friendly comrades brought many rewards to our life and a tremendous sense of comfort and belonging.

In October 2013 Connie and I moved to Lake Seminole near Donalsonville, Georgia desiring to live our final years among long-time friends and relatives. We found a home on a water front lot with a boat dock which would support our love of nature and my love of fishing. What a joy to walk into restaurants and businesses seeing friends and relatives with whom we could visit, a stark contrast to the city.

At this point in our lives, we are happier than we have ever been with love that grows deeper in spite of challenges that life has bestowed on us. Our membership in the Friendship Methodist Church in Donalsonville rounds out our life with friends present every Sunday and a feeling of love throughout. We are thankful for our many blessings.

CHAPTER 44

RED HEAD

As Connie and I reached forty years of age, our desire for parent-hood approached a new high. The window was closing which made us think longer and harder about whether we wanted a child. Previously, Connie had never wanted children, so being ambivalent I had not pushed the issue, but she had recently developed an interest in being a mother that had easily pulled me along.

Having fertility examinations, Connie appeared without flaws in her reproductive system while I was diagnosed with a problem. The chief issue being my little swimmers preferred to sit on the bank, drink beer and watch television than go after the egg. The doctor said these guys appeared too deeply into their lifestyle for them ever to become interested in exercise so I accepted my fate.

After discussing it thoroughly, with apprehension we decided to look into artificial insemination. The fertility doctor said that the do-nors were medical school students so that allayed some of our fears. With us being provided a background profile of a possible donor, he appeared acceptable without any history of diseases or conditions. So we gave it a shot and hoped for success, but the one-time procedure failed, so we gave up. Connie was forty-three years old and had entered that birth-risk period of her life. We certainly did not want to confront any of the potential birth defects associated with late-in-life pregnancies.

Now we were in a position of looking into adoption or reconciling our minds to remaining childless, which we could have accepted without remorse.

As providence would have it, Connie had a friend at work who had a sister in Chicago that wanted to give up a child when born. Her friend spoke with the sister and determined that there was an interest in offering the child to us for private adoption. Based on the informal agreement, we started the wheels turning to make it happen.

Totally ignorant of adoption, we began asking questions and learning. This would be a private adoption, therefore the state of Colorado would intrude into our business.

Contacting an adoption agency which handled these transactions, we delved into the steps, some ridiculous, that were required to adopt a child. One representative from the agency handled our case's paperwork and interviews. Noting the complexity involved, I had to wonder of the potential loving parents who walked away after understanding the cumbersome and expensive process.

The interviews went well with an expression of concern about our "support system" as if we would have to be bailed out should we come into circumstances of not being able to support the child financially or otherwise. At that point in our lives, about the only support system we had would have been Connie's family though her father had passed away a couple years previous. We gave enough information to satisfy our caseworker, so that hurdle had been passed.

The expenses attached to this adoption alarmed us. We had to pay for the adoption agency fees, the delivery expenses at the hospital and for psychological counseling for the birth mother to ensure that adoption suited her. Other smaller expenses of flying to Chicago, a motel room, a lawyer fee and miscellaneous state fees brought the total to about $15,000. This happened in 1986 so the outlay currently must be huge. Were we adopting a child or buying one?

Plunging ahead one afternoon in late August 1986, we flew to Chicago to become instant parents. The rules had required that we not take the child into our possession until two weeks after the birth, so the child had to spend that time with the birth mother which could have caused second thoughts that would have halted the process. We had valid worries but saw no choice but to live with the rules considering the money we had spent so far was at risk.

We went to a Catholic agency which assisted with these kinds of transactions to find the infant girl and her birth mother. As we walked in, we saw a lovely twenty-six year old red-headed, smiling mother holding a carrot-topped, beautiful girl. The instant I saw them I sensed that this exchange was going to be tough on the three of us.

After visiting a few minutes with the mother, expressing our thanks and learning about the child and its routine, the time had come for the passing of the child from the young lady's arms into Connie's. As the infant was passed between them, the emotions took control and tears flowed. Connie and I felt strong empathy for this woman who had the courage to do what she thought was best for the child. The birth mother cried because of the finality of what had just happened. This child that she had carried for nine months, birthed and nursed for the last two weeks was leaving the room with new parents. We thanked her for trusting us and wished her luck, then we walked out the door.

We named her Jacklyn Samantha Harman Mills, extracting the Jacklyn from Connie's father Jack, the Sam in Samantha from me and the Harman from Connie's birth name. Over a period of time, Harman has been dropped from use and Jacklyn has been shortened to a nickname of Jackie.

If ever there were a doting, helicopter mother, Connie fit that mold perfectly. She and I were both delighted to have this darling in our family.

Since my niece had lost a child to SIDS, Connie insisted that we purchase a baby monitor which would broadcast her sounds to our bedroom and downstairs. It included an electronic apparatus which attached to her chest that monitored her heartbeat, sounding an alarm if it were interrupted. This was an early-generation technology which gave false alarms that caused many unwarranted runs to her baby crib.

As Jackie grew, we purchased a video camera that we used extensively. The first years of her life were well documented, luckily catching her first steps. She did not ease into walking. When she started, she walked continuously. Eventually putting the movies on DVD's, Jackie now has them to show her child one day.

It would be fair to say that Jackie was spoiled. I did a fine job of it but Connie made me look like a piker. I used to kid her about buying the "toy of the day." Jackie would grab a toy in a store, and Connie would bring it home. Not an appropriate habit with us eventually having to address the excesses.

Loving Jackie dearly, we had become mentally prepared to handle any obstacles that arose. Noticing that Jackie had a difficult time being still, recognizing the word "no" and being prone to temper fits, we became aware that we had to find help as she grew up.

Receiving two separate diagnoses of ADHD, we put her on prescribed drugs. As other children, she did not like how they made her feel. By the time she reached the age of about thirteen, she resisted taking the pills. With the meds having helped her focus on school studies, her grades suffered additionally than they already were suffering.

As she went into her teen years, she became rebellious and caused us alarm for the path she could be taking. A counselor in Panama City, Florida, determined that Jackie had what was known then as attachment disorder. The disorder caused oppositional and defiant behaviors, disrespect for those around her, a control personality and an obsession to test the limits of whatever kept her from satisfying selfish goals.

We learned that ADHD was just a subset of attachment disorder. The root cause of attachment disorder is separation from a birth mother. Though we got her at only two weeks of age, her brain had gone through a trauma, detecting that there had been separation from the birth mother.

Observing that we were desperate to find a way to help Jackie, the counselor suggested an organization near Denver, Colorado, that specialized in children with attachment disorder. They had a two-week program that was an intervention which diminished the effects of the disorder. It was expensive, but we saw no other alternative for addressing her issues.

For two weeks we and Jackie, at age fifteen, attended counseling sessions with a specially trained psychologist in the mornings Monday through Friday. After lunch, we dropped Jackie off with a "mother from hell" who had a nearby home with her husband. She became a surrogate mother as Jackie stayed with her each afternoon following counseling and each night with us picking her up the next morning. Other children with similar disorders stayed at the couple's home, a disciplined setting that taught the kids that their actions had consequences.

Leaving Jackie there and driving away was rough on her and us, but we knew it was best. Toward the end of the first week, I sensed a change in Jackie when she told us to be careful on the way home. That was the first time she had ever cared about our welfare. The counselor said that Jackie had never bonded with us, so this was beginning evidence of bonding.

When the two weeks were over, we were exhausted. The counseling sessions were extremely intense, being so taxing for us to watch the analyst delve deeply into Jackie's psyche. It was apparent that Jackie had been "moved" in a positive direction.

Through the rest of high school and an attempt at college, Jackie was a difficult child. Not losing control of her was our significant accomplishment. She did not run away from home, become a drug addict or alcoholic, get pregnant nor spend time in jail. The baggage that she came into life with did not pull her totally down.

Reading that generally children acquire their parent's values by the age of thirty, I feel confident that Jackie is on track for that accomplishment. At age twenty eight, she has a darling one year old boy, Dominic and a loving partner, Antonio Dibacco. Jackie is still trying to sort out her life, expressing an interest in returning to college.

Having had our lumps and bumps with Jackie, we have always helped and protected her from the harshest consequences of life. We love her and are proud that she and her family are a part of our lives.

CHAPTER 45

SISTER

Varying portions of strife enter people's lives. Some individuals escape with a fairy tale existence while others receive their share plus an additional amount. My sister received way beyond a fairly-assessed slice of difficult times. She stood up well under the load until she had to bury children. At that point it became unbearable.

Cut from a similar mold as I was, Sister, as we called her, had well learned how to take care of whatever life dealt. When people are raised tough and have to struggle, they do not shrink away from the challenges of life. They confront them head-on and do what it takes to overcome obstacles.

A poignant memory of her in our cotton patch wearing a black hat and working as the males in our family brings sadness when I bounce it around in my grey matter. I was only five or six years old when that recollection decided to reside between my ears but it left an impression. I felt sorry for her. In my mind at that tender age, picking cotton was a task we males did. My sister should not have had to do that type of work but should have been in the house helping Mama.

Being from the last class to graduate from Seminole County High School with a total of eleven years secondary education, she finished in 1951 at the age of sixteen. Certainly mature beyond her years, she headed off to Tallahassee, Florida, and a job as a typist in a state office building. She fared well with her city job, fit in well and liked her new home.

At age eighteen Sister married a full-blooded Cherokee Indian, a warm and handsome guy whom she loved dearly. Our family liked Coy Sketo, a loving, devoted husband. Within five years they had two girls and a boy which completed their family.

In 1962 roughly eight years after their marriage, Coy was diagnosed with incurable kidney disease. Dying at the age of thirty, he only lived six or eight months after they learned the troubling news. With no dialysis available, kidney patients wasted away without hope. I remember attending the funeral in Tallahassee in November 1962, such a sad event for Sister, the three children, our family and friends.

Between social security help for the children and her job, Sister at age twenty-eight was able to stay afloat financially and keep their modest home. She was the strong trooper that we knew her to be and did not let the circumstances pull her down.

Less than a year afterward, she started dating a gentleman eight years her junior with their marriage in 1963. Our family was concerned with the speed at which that happened, the influence the three kids could have on the marriage and the disparity in their ages. Knowing her strength and convictions, we trusted her to produce the right decision.

In March 1964 the couple had a son, the only offspring of their marriage. This addition completed the family and solidified the marriage — for about fifteen years. From our family's observations they had a happy, thriving marriage, but apparently there were concerns hidden from our sight.

Circa 1979 Sister divorced her husband and moved from their residence in Tennessee back to Tallahassee. By this time the first three children were grown and the youngest was age fifteen. Sister went back to work for the State of Florida in its Corrections Division. Also, she obtained a part time job at Gayfer's department store as a sales associate in the china department.

No stranger to work, for the next seventeen years, she toiled forty hours a week on her state job and twenty hours a week at her other job to maintain the life she wanted. She bought a modest home in Tallahassee and enjoyed being single with devotion to her children filling her life. Possessing a strong mother instinct, she loved the children dearly and would help them in any way she could.

The next wave of disappointment began in the early '80s when her oldest daughter Melinda was diagnosed with kidney disease. By this time Melinda had a husband and two children with the family residing in Tennessee.

Laboring over the diagnosis, the doctors determined that the disease was extremely rare, so rare it did not have a name. They suspected that Melinda had received the malady through her father's genes. Applying known treatments to no avail, the doctors eventually had to put her on dialysis.

About 1985 Melinda's brother Ben started having abnormal creatinine levels and was diagnosed with the same disease in its earlier stages. As in Melinda's case, high blood pressure was involved in the deterioration of his kidneys. Ben continued to work on his traveling sales job with the King Edward cigar company but experienced health setbacks of tiredness, hypertension and other complications.

In July 1987 I received a call that Ben was in Loma Linda hospital in California in a life- threatening condition attributable to a brain aneurism. I flew that afternoon to California since I had become close to Ben with him being almost like a son to me.

The next day the doctors operated to repair the aneurism, but Ben died hours later because of complications. Apparently there was a congenital weakness in an artery of the brain, and his high blood pressure had precipitated the rupture.

Ben left a wife Anna, a one year old daughter Brittney and a four year old son Brian.

Ben's loss took a toll on Sister. She had a dead son and a daughter suffering with the same disease. With kidney disease the side effects and other complications destroy lives, not just the lives of those afflicted but also those who love them.

Circa 1993 after a year plus on dialysis, Melinda passed away at the age of about thirty-seven of heart disease, a complication of the kidney condition. Melinda left her husband with two children, Lindsey about ten years old and Stephen fifteen.

Sister had lost two children, both with families and in what should have been the prime of their lives. She was especially close to Melinda, so the pain of the loss wore terribly.

At Melinda's passing, her sister Sharlyn was already suffering with the same disease. Sharlyn eventually had two kidney transplants, neither of which was successful. Sharlyn, passing in 2005 at the age of 45, suffered for about fifteen years before she succumbed to the disease. She left a son Josh, a daughter Jacoby and a husband. Josh died in 2005 in his mid-twenties from a drug overdose. Apparently a doctor had recently identified a raised creatinine level in his blood.

Having developed hypertension, Sister's health started deteriorating after Melinda's death. In January 1997 she had open heart surgery including bypasses of diseased arteries. A stroke happened during or after the surgery that left her with a partially paralyzed arm and hand.

Ironically, Sister took a trip September 1997 to Texas to visit her son Geno and wife and on to Memphis to see Connie, Jackie and me. Sharlyn lived not far away, so we drove there and spent part of a day with her and family. Sister stayed two or three nights with us and flew back on a Friday to Tallahassee.

The next morning after arriving back she had poured a cup of coffee and set it on a table in her living room. Performing her morning routine, she went to retrieve her newspaper near the curb and fell in her front yard on the way back to the house. A neighbor noticed her lying near her front door and alerted emergency personnel. Sister had died about the time she had fallen.

The death certificate probably mentioned a heart condition as the cause of death. Knowing her and how she loved her children, I would offer that she died from a broken heart. Considering the two lost children and having a third child with kidney disease, Sister's heart had carried a heavy, unsustainable load.

Unfortunately, the unyielding disease had not finished with the Coy Sketo descendants. Circa 2008 Melinda's son Stephen was stricken at about age twenty-eight and diagnosed when he had fifty percent of his kidney function remaining. Over the years the doctors had learned that rapidly advancing hypertension was the culprit that destroyed the kidneys. With the hypertension under control, presently Stephen has a promising future and is apparently in good health.

In about 2010 Ben's son Brian was stricken with the same disease. He had only about twenty five percent kidney capacity remaining when diagnosed so he had a legitimate threat to his life. Eventually he had to be on dialysis for about three years before having a transplant. In the summer of 2014, his mother donated a kidney to help Brian receive one from a donor who would be a match for him. His surgery was a success and Brian seems to be doing well and expecting a normal life span.

The year 2014 came to be a blessed year for the Sketo descendants. Sharlyn's daughter Jacoby had contracted the disease and was diagnosed in late 2012. Having only about thirty percent kidney capacity remaining when diagnosed, she needed a transplant soon, or she would have to do dialysis.

As fate would have it, in May 2014 Jacoby received a kidney transplant from a first cousin on her father's side of the family. What a blessing that was! She is doing well and has regained weight and health she lost while in peril. With a job in the country music management business and a marriage scheduled in March 2016, she has a bright future. Her job has afforded the chance of rubbing shoulders with the famous in the music business.

Two of my sister's granddaughters, Lindsey and Brittney, are the only ones who have not contracted the disease. Lindsey is past thirty years old and probably safe since the disease has attacked routinely before that age. Brittney will be twenty-nine years of age on her next birthday in July 2015. Hopefully she has dodged the gene and the disease will not attack her.

Steadfastly, medical science is gaining the upper hand with the disease. I still find it difficult to think about Sister and her descendants knowing the grief and pain they have suffered. Whenever the subject of life being fair, or not, comes up, I rest assured that their outcomes were a grand example of the unfairness life can deliver.

Time will reveal whether the disorder continues in future generations. Stephen is the parent of two young girls, Lindsey has a boy and a girl and Brittney is the mother of a young boy. Neither Brian nor Jacoby are married yet. Chances are this inheritable disease will appear again, but the better medical care of this era is on their side.

CHAPTER 46

MERCIES

Of the deep, personal interactions a person may have in life, the number one maintenance priority is that relationship with God because without Him other aspects of people's lives have less meaning. Bits and pieces of religion, which planted a seed that was a long time sprouting, started rubbing off on me in my childhood.

Daddy would say the unintelligible blessing at meals and often refer to God as "The Old Master." According to him, The Old Master brought rain from St. Peters Pond when our crops were starting to burn in the fields. When not drinking, Daddy led an honest and honorable life and to my knowledge did not do unkind things on purpose to anyone. I probably did not see him in church a half dozen times in my childhood, but he had a relationship with God that was solid.

Mama wore her religion proudly out front for the whole world to see. Having joined the Rock Pond Primitive Baptist church when she was about forty-five years old, she put her heart into religion and her relationship with God. Witnessing the genuine love in the church among the members, I could tell that she experienced something I had not tapped into in my youth.

Toward the end of each service the members gathered near the pulpit and hugged each other in fellowship. They enjoyed dinner on the grounds as a means of further enriching the relationships with each other and God. Watching these interactions gave me appreciation for the love of fellow man.

In day to day challenges, she would often mention God and ask Him to bless the family with His Grace. She seemed to look frequently to Him for guidance in finding the right course to take.

Mother, being a member of the church, never pushed any of her children to become members. My two brothers did not join a church. Sister became a member when past the age of forty, and I joined at about sixty years old. Finding a relationship of commitment with the Lord at a young age would have been best, but it did not happen with us siblings.

Possessing an engineering mind and a quest to recognize the "reasonable and rational" of my environment, I was able to see God around me wherever I chose to look. The orderliness and complexities of nature and the universe convinced me that there had to be a higher power involved in their creation and sustainment. The ornate colors, beauty and intricacies of design of birds, animals and plants were testimony to the involvement of divine guidance. The biological systems that work together in concert to propagate and maintain the various species could not have happened in random acts.

Circa 2004 after introspective thinking and laboring over the decision, I knew that the time was right for me to commit to God. Connie had joined the Lutheran Church in Watertown, South Dakota, in her youth and had progressed to a position of Sunday school teacher for the younger children in her congregation. With a gentle nudge, Connie came on board to join the Lynn Haven Florida United Methodist Church.

In spite of Connie's youthful beginnings in the church, after she left home at age eighteen, she had wandered away from religion and not participated for over forty years. She and her two sisters, growing up in the church, had strayed after leaving home. Something had been amiss in the way religion had been brought into their lives so when of age they had abandoned it. Connie had bitterness regarding the church's not allowing her to be a member of the Girl Scouts, and there had been other undetermined issues which she had in common with her sisters.

With friends from our neighborhood being in the church, our making it a part of our lives seemed natural. After Sunday services, a group of us would gather for breakfast or brunch to enjoy the fellowship. Connie and I felt better inside from participating in the Sunday rituals and feeling the presence of Him.

With many ministries as most churches, LH Methodist sponsored the building of ramps for those confined to manual and powered wheel chairs. Being interested in contributing to the ministry, I inquired of the group leader Tom Gildersleeve of how I might participate. He said to show up in the parking lot of the church at 7:00 a.m. on Saturdays and join the group.

Tom stood out among unusual characters with whom I had the pleasure of association. Past seventy years old with a white mustache and sporting a rotund stomach which spilled over his belt attributable to his love of confections, he was the most laid back, even tempered disciple of God that I had ever known. When things went wrong on a project, his demeanor remained the same as when we were blessed with things happening without a hitch. Everyone knew he was in charge, not by his authority, but by his commitment to the job. He listened to the senior men around him with decisions being made so effortlessly we could often wonder if a decision had been made.

He was Lynn Haven Methodist Church's "Saint of Ramps," and I am satisfied that he has a special place reserved with Him when his service on Earth is finished.

Having been a "shade tree" carpenter in my retirement, I saw this as a chance to use and to grow my skills for a worthwhile purpose.

Each Saturday ten church members, plus or minus, dependent on other Saturday obligations, showed up to build an access ramp.

Well-seasoned seniors comprised the core of the construction crew with younger, less skilled members helping with whatever they could contribute. There were always boards to carry and holes to dig which required a modicum of skill or training. The average age of the seniors was probably at least seventy, so we had an abundance of know-how and skills on the projects.

Moving out of the parking lot in a caravan with Tom driving an old van pulling a flat twelve-foot trailer containing wood and tools we would need, we traveled to our customer's house in five or six vehicles to do an installation. Sometimes traveling as far as fifteen or twenty miles, we looked forward to making a handicapped person's life easier.

On arrival at our client's house, Tom went to the door and told the resident that we were there and on the job while the rest of us unloaded the lumber and tools positioning them in the proper location for convenient access during construction. An associate found a power outlet and plugged in a long extension cord with a surge protector for supplying power to the various pieces of equipment.

The team effort to put together a twenty-five to thirty foot ramp in three to four hours was exemplary. Setting to work like an army of ants building a new hill, the work went smoothly with few obstructions encountered. Team members started sawing and joining the two by tens we used as the basic bottom structure. After that was assembled, we attached it to a front porch with "header boards." Occasionally we had to rework the porches by taking out pieces of railing or repairing portions of the porch's structure to ensure we had a good base for attaching the ramp.

With manual hole-diggers we dug holes along the sides of the ramp for placement of support posts. When inserting the four by four support posts in the holes, we added cement to ensure stability of the structure.

After the posts were positioned and attached to the ramp, our group nailed down the ramp boards on which the wheelchairs would ride. We sawed off the posts to the proper height to accommodate the ramp's incline and attached safety railings to the posts. Near completion one of our group would use an electric wood grinder to buff away any splinters that might protrude on boards which a user could touch.

Lastly, our group went inside to pray with and for our customer. Tom or one of the seniors of the group always led the prayer which was needed and appreciated given the circumstances. These people we helped had difficult lives. Usually they were advanced in age, and often there had been an incurable diagnosis.

In excess of ninety percent of occurrences, the client lived in an older manufactured home. Seeing the conditions in which some lived caused us to thank the Lord for our blessings.

Being retired, I often received calls from Tom during the week since he became involved in people's other needs besides wheelchair ramps. We would install handicap bars in bathrooms, fix front doors that would not lock, repair floors in homes that had rotted away, do partial renovation of a bathroom to make it functional and perform various plumbing work. In one case I remember raw sewage dumping on the ground beneath a house, so we reconnected a sewage line to a cesspool to solve that problem.

This work was done in the middle of the hot summers or the cooler winters. Many times I returned home with my clothes soaked from sweat or chilled from the North Florida wind in January. Just watching Tom work, being ten years my senior, caused me to stifle any complaints of conditions.

Of the people I had worked with in my career the wheelchair ministry team was the finest by any measure. If I could have worked with that caliber of temperament and conviction in my career, I would not be taking acid reflux pills presently. They were not just good people;

they were exceptional. The rewarding work we did complemented my life and provided a sense of pride in doing valuable work.

Having both back and hip pain, I had to give up the job after about three years and helping build about a hundred ramps. Since then, I have had bone spurs removed from both hips and arthroscopic surgery on my back. Both were successful with praise to God.

CHAPTER 47

STUMPS

A s we advance in age, incidents involve us that we should have been wise to avoid, but unknowingly the foibles come looking for us who should have long passed that level of ignorance. In the spring of 2009, at the ages of sixty-three, my high school buddy Terry Ingram and I pursued our favorite pastime, fishing in Lake Seminole. With a water temperature of fifty-three degrees, we plundered stumps west of the Chattahoochee and a couple miles from the Jim Woodruff dam searching for crappie.

We had a routine of easing through the stumps with Terry standing up front watching carefully, giving me hand signals to avoid the sturdy protrusions which were green and healthy trees fifty years ago when the dam was constructed and the trees flooded. As we threaded our way through the stumps, we had committed two unfortunate acts: Terry standing up in the boat and his not wearing a life jacket.

Constantly searching the area in front of the boat for stumps which were exposed and for those visible stumps inches below the water surface, Terry's job was to prevent any mishaps. The taller ones could tip the boat and the shorter ones could cause the boat to become wedged on top of them. For an unknown reason, Terry did not see a stump protruding three to five inches above the water.

As the boat road up on the stump, striking the boat bottom to the left of the boat's center, the vessel tilted right and I stopped the engine. Performing a ninety degree spin counterclockwise, Terry fell off the right side of the boat on his back. Struggling back to the top of the water, he instinctively grabbed for the boat which was tilted about thirty degrees in his direction. Shifting his weight to the boat's side to re-enter caused water to come in which brought alarm to me, and I yelled, "You cannot get in there. You will sink us. Go to the rear of the boat."

Having added weight over the years, Terry struggled along the side of the boat to the back with me suggesting that he stand on the foot of the motor with one foot to gain leverage for stepping back into the vessel. Placing his right foot on the motor, he could not gain maneuverable traction. Asking him what was wrong, he responded, "I lost my right shoe and the sock is too slippery." Perturbed and disgustedly realizing that shoes were the least of our obstacles, he pulled off his other shoe and tossed it away

Taking a brief assessment of our jam, I noticed that Terry had labored breathing and a pale complexion which alarmed me. The exercise of treading water and hanging onto the boat along with the cold water temperature were taking a toll. With the clock ticking toward possible disaster, we had a time limitation necessitating bold action.

Setting my brain to work on a way of freeing him from the frigid water, I thought of the boat anchor with its electric wench recognizing that there was one at the back of the boat near him. I told Terry that I would drop the anchor far enough down into the water that he could position his foot on it. Then I would raise the anchor and him to a point where he could jump into the boat. Negating that suggestion, he said, "That won't work. It's not strong enough to handle me." Both of us knew that his weight would put severe strain on the anchor motor.

Growing paler and colder with my concern peaking, he paddled around the back of the boat for two-three minutes. We had to remove him from the water soon, or I would need to tie a rope around him for dragging him to shallow water.

Revisiting the consideration of the anchor pulling him out, I asked him again, "Remember that plan of you standing on the anchor? Want to try it now?" Convinced by extra time in that cold hell, he was in favor of using the idea. With desperation in his voice, he said, "Let's try it." I dropped the anchor for him to stand on its surface with one foot which was all it could accommodate. With me bringing up the anchor, he rose to a point where he could lunge into the back corner of the boat. As he made his move, the anchor reset and stopped, but he made a successful landing. We were both relieved. Since he was totally exhausted and in the throes of hypothermia, he lay in the back of the boat for about ten minutes regaining his oxygen and rejoicing in being out of that torment.

Additional water came into the boat during his retrieval but the volume was not a threat. The first thing I did was back the boat off the stump and engage the bilge pump to remove the quantity of water in the vessel. The pump ran most of the way back home disposing of more water than I had imagined.

The altercation had caused our minnow buckets to turn over and to scatter our tackle boxes and other paraphernalia around. As I started to clear the clutter in the boat, I noticed a life cushion which I could have tossed to Terry in his dire need. In the midst of catastrophe, a partial fog had invaded my brain.

The steering position required the driver to be in the back of the boat leaving no location for Terry but the front and full exposure to the wind for the four mile ride back to my house. Extremely cold, he shivered the distance back dreaming of a hot shower to regain body heat.

When reaching the house, he stripped and went into the shower where he stayed so long, I yelled at him to see if he was okay. The near disaster had ended our fishing trip.

Today we can laugh about the accident and our lack of good judgment. Terry nor I ever left the dock again without lifejackets securely cinched. I was so thankful we came out of that one alive and well. Calling his wife Ellen and reporting his demise would have been a difficult task. Thanks to the Lord for sparing us.

CHAPTER 48

A DEAR FRIEND

Passing away September 18, 2014, at the age of 84, Betty Miller Ausley, wife of my first cousin Slim, lived a full life. She had more than her share of fun including an abundance of memorable times and friends with whom she shared life's joys and heartaches. Betty, a certified original, was different from anyone I have ever known with no one closely resembling her in character and personality.

Having her passions: family, gardening, cooking, fishing and socializing with those whom she loved and who loved her, she always had her days filled. Doing nothing half-way, her heart was always in her interests one hundred percent.

About 1999 she and my brother Lloyd found opportunities to fish together in spite of their unexplained relationship. Having strong, irrevocable views on a multitude of passionate subjects, they readily shared their opinions at a moment's notice whether the listener wanted to hear them or not. With Lloyd and Betty seeing only black and white, no shades of grey existed in their worlds. Often expressing themselves with emotions and words that made friends and acquaintances feel uncomfortable, both had skin an inch thick and considered others' hides equally as durable. At the time he was about sixty-four and she about seventy in age.

Perhaps fishing was a way for them to escape from others and let their hair down along with their thoughts. Surrounded by God's nature, no one could be offended except perhaps the alligators at Lake Seminole who probably knew not to get into an argument with either of them.

Their outings could have been a one-sided hollering contest since Lloyd could not hear well. Of course, he did not listen well in his earlier days when he could hear. His hearing had been diminished by exposure to shotguns and tractor engines over the years. They caught a few fish, shared old stories, had animated "discussions," and enjoyed each's company apparently.

On a summer's day they went to Lake Seminole to catch pan fish as they had done often. Little did they suspect that as Lloyd backed the boat and trailer down the ramp a surprise waited for them.

With Lloyd stopping the boat at the edge of the water, they both went back to the boat to do prep tasks: putting items in the boat that they had in the truck, undoing the tie-down straps and checking to ensure the drain plug remained engaged.

Their routine of launching the boat was the same as they had used on each occasion. Lloyd would climb into the boat and prepare to start it while she would back the trailer deeper into the water until the boat floated free. Betty would park the boat and trailer as he pulled up to the dock to wait for her to board.

Having climbed into the boat, Lloyd waved at Betty that he was in the driver's seat and ready for her to back up. Cautiously, she backed up a few additional feet, and the boat began floating off the trailer.

The spinning of the crank on the trailer gave Lloyd his first hint that their day had trouble afoot. Attached to the crank was the nylon strap which connected to the hook that secured the boat when "trailered". When untrailering the boat, the boater must unhook from the "tow ring" on the front of the boat.

Lacking thoroughness, they had missed a "foolish detail" and the boat remained attached to the trailer. Betty gunned the truck and began charging out of the water as the crank kept spinning, so in an instant the remainder of the strap unraveled which gave Lloyd a sharp jerk in his seat. Immediately panicking, he screamed and yelled as loud as he could, "Stop! Stop!"

Betty, focused on her job of parking the truck and trailer, did not hear the yelling nor look back. First the trailer came out of the water and following close behind was Lloyd in the boat. When the boat ran out of water to ride in, it started scrapping along on the asphalt parking lot. Oblivious of Lloyd's plight, Betty continued on her mission to park, and Lloyd screamed his displeasure with higher decibels.

After towing her load for ten or fifteen yards, Betty either heard a noise or looked back and saw Lloyd's red face in the mirror which caused her to apply the brakes. Captain Lloyd's "dry land cruise" finally came to a screeching halt.

Alarmed, Betty jumped out of the truck and ran back to the boat. Before she could say a word, Lloyd calmly said, "Hand me a fishing pole, Betty. I think they might be biting right here." Betty's sense of humor had gone on vacation. If the truth were known, she handed him a pole — the butt end of it.

Being aware of their personalities, I can rest assured that neither of them took credit for the calamity. Sharp words from both directions drowned out any possibility of diplomacy or logical thinking. Blaming time had arrived and their shortest fishing trip had ended with zero catch.

Over the years the story of how they got that boat back on the trailer in the parking lot was not told to me though obviously assistance was required. Lifting a sixteen foot boat with a forty horse motor requires a quantity of muscles or creative thinking.

If an observer could have been sitting in a tree with a video camera, he could have captured antics as good as or better than any of

Bill Dance's bloopers. Likewise, a fly on the wall in that truck on the way home could have gotten a lesson in reverse diplomacy.

Friendship and family withstood, and they remained friends after this mishap. Relishing arguing with each other, they looked forward to future disagreements.

Betty will be missed forever by those who had the good fortune of being her friend. Always enjoying taking her fish to eat in the last few years, I would listen to fishing tales involving her late husband or perhaps stories of the fun people they knew years ago. Rest in peace, Betty. What a run — a robust, lively one!

CHAPTER 49

A TESTIMONIAL TO THE POWER OF GOD

God has answered our prayers so Connie and I feel we should share the path He has provided for us in His Name. When we look at the sequence of events that brought us to our present circumstances, divine guidance is the only explanation. Random chance nor applied human guidance can explain the many favorable choices and occurrences. When we look at each step we took, there was high probability of failure for each. When we allow for the probabilities of failure at each step to arrive at the odds of them happening in combination, the probabilities are huge. God listened to our prayers.

In 2008 our family doctor Myra Reed of Panama City Beach, Florida, agreed that Connie had a brain dysfunction and ordered blood tests to diagnose what deficiencies could affect memory. Her internal organs had healthy function, but the blood analysis indicated vitamin D and folic acid deficiencies plus borderline anemia, nothing at a level to cause dementia.

After about six months of blood tests and follow up, Dr. Reed referred us to a neurologist who suspected a form of dementia, probably Alzheimer's, and prescribed the medications, Donepezil and Namenda which hide some of the symptoms of dementia for a period of time. Being the caregiver, I observed improvements, but the meds did not offer a long term solution. The doctor had an office which resembled semi-organized chaos causing us to feel we had not found the best medical treatment.

We were referred to a neurologist in Tallahassee, Florida. Neither did this doctor impress us, but he had an important point to offer. He said that we should obtain a thorough diagnosis, noting that her memory problem could be Alzheimer's or another of many forms of dementia. For Connie to have a possibility of being treated, we had to obtain a proper diagnosis.

He referred us to the Mayo Clinic in Jacksonville, Florida, which proved to be a meaningful step toward gaining a diagnosis. After two appointments including extensive interviews and testing, the neurologist concluded that Connie had Alzheimer's with a ninety percent probability, a medical opinion we found troublesome to accept.

My education, being of a technical nature, told me that we should obtain confirmation of those findings, so our Tallahassee doctor referred us to Shands Clinic in Gainesville, Florida with interviews and testing indicating the same ninety percent probability of Alzheimer's. The only known method of having one hundred percent certitude is an autopsy.

Surgeries to remove bone spurs from my hips in September and December of 2010 had slowed me down, but I was back on the problem of how to help Connie after a period of therapy and recovery in 2011. The diagnosis I found unsettling considering the disease guaranteed the death of the patient in a period of years. The alternative of doing nothing had no space in my brain, so I began reading about research on the internet.

For several months in the late summer and fall of 2011, I researched Alzheimer's clinical trials on the internet. Dedicated thinking and studying led me to the conclusion that comprehensive research to fight the disease was underway in this country and others. The reading of internet articles suggested hope for a breakthrough within five years which triggered me to conclude that we should become a part of research, not only to reap any benefits for Connie, but to help others who already had or may contract the dreaded affliction.

When starting down this path, I had no understanding of clinical trials, of how they worked nor of how to enroll in one. Day after day for over a month, I sat at my computer reviewing studies on clinical-trials.gov, a site which listed trials for a number of diseases, whether they were open for participation, the location of the clinical studies and specifics of requirements for being accepted in the studies. The location of the trials carried importance since we would have to commute, but in desperation I considered sites as far as 500 miles away. The drugs being tested and the drug company names gave me information for further research on the internet. In most cases articles had been published of the drugs' merits, failures and potential. When we committed to a clinical trial, it needed to have the potential of beneficial results.

Finding an acceptable clinical trial became my goal and my obsession. The Alzheimer's Association helped determine if a study was still open for enrollment and would give me leads and phone numbers of clinics to call. Clinicaltrials.gov, not well maintained in 2011, had old information on some trials that proved meaningless. Amazingly, doctors provided no help or info on clinical trials, probably attributable to them requiring their valuable time.

Using the criteria of the drugs' potential and geographic proximity, frustration hit me head-on. A portion of studies that offered favorable criteria had been closed for participation while others presented a commuting challenge. After months of investigation, I finally settled on one workable candidate, DeKalb Neurology in

Decatur, Georgia, studying Bapineuzumab, an Eli Lilly drug, which had complimentary articles on the internet. The clinic was looking for Alzheimer's patients who did not have the ApoE4 gene, but testing detected its presence in Connie's system. What a downer! But in my disappointment God had other plans.

We spoke with Dr. Nash to understand what could be a next step, and he mentioned the drug Crenezumab which his clinic had in Phase II testing, sponsored by Genentech. Being unfamiliar with the drug, I asked Dr. Nash to give us guidance on what to do. He stated that he would choose Crenezumab over Bapineuzumab because, "Genentech makes some cool drugs." Those words and the way he said them brought us to a better state of mind.

We did not give him an answer, traveling home for me to do independent research of the drug on the internet. With the hype for Crenezumab being less than the publicity for the Eli Lilly drug, God told us to accept Dr. Nash's recommendation.

From December 2011 until October 2014, we made biweekly trips to the Decatur clinic. During the period, Genentech was generous to us by paying our motel bills, mileage and funding monitoring of Connie's health to guard against potential unwanted reactions. Dr. Nash and his team had been diligent at administering the drug, carefully collecting data and protecting Connie's health. She had been given a brain MRI every six months with the clinician stating there was no change in the last three MRI's which was grand news but not totally indicative of changes in mental capabilities.

Unfortunately for Eli Lilly's drug, Bapineuzumab, the Phase II studies were cancelled within a year after we started the Genentech study because of not producing expected results. God had steered us to the better drug, Crenezumab.

In May 2010 we had gone to Brent Decker, PHD in Panama City, Florida, for extensive testing to establish a baseline for monitoring Connie's progress or lack of it. Returning in May 2013, his findings disclosed insignificant net brain deterioration during the period.

Select portions of the brain's capabilities had decreased and others had improved. We were excited that her IQ had remained the same, being the most important indicator of brain stability. We have another session scheduled in June 2015 to continue the monitoring of her capabilities.

In October 2014 we received news from the clinic that administering the drug by IV increased its effectiveness versus the injections she had been given to that point. When they told us that we should come every four weeks rather than every two, we were ecstatic. God bestowed double blessings on us. Then, they shared some unwanted news that Phase II of the study would end in January 2015 which left us in a quandary. What would we do without the hope the medicine had given us and its benefits? Would there be a Phase III study?

God had not finished with His good news. In December 2014 the head nurse told us that Genentech had extended the Phase II study until May 2016 which precipitated my asking a question. Did this decision indicate that the drug had promise? The nurse confirmed that it did, which was overwhelming to us.

In 2013 Crenezumab was chosen among twenty-five competing drugs to be used in a study of an extended family in Columbia, South America. Since family members had been diagnosed with Alzheimer's as early as age thirty-five, the research group wanted to test the drug's prevention properties.

Realizing that Connie has been stable for at least five years, I declared, "It's never over until God says it is." God has given us the strength and commitment to fight Alzheimer's, and He has guided us in the right direction when there were many opportunities to choose the wrong fork in the road. All praise to our Lord. We thank Him each day for his Grace and Blessings.

EPILOGUE

The two variables of time and place are critical in any human experience. When by luck of the draw the two entities complement each other, rewarding results can be forthcoming.

Being born in 1945 in Seminole County, Georgia, I regard as being among my top ten blessings. For this old sharecropper's son to be able to make that statement knowing that I have been blessed in so many ways is a blessing, also.

Knowing the past of our country and fearful for the future, I feel so fortunate to have been born in that period. I would argue that 1945 is smack dab in the middle of the golden age of coming into being. Those individuals born between 1935 and 1960 experienced our country in the best of times. The times were so good that people who experienced the benefits can now wonder if that was as good as it could get.

Having never drawn a welfare check or unemployment check or been without the wherewithal to live happily, I have been a beneficiary of 1945 and Seminole County. The lessons, the values, the love and the help associated with growing up where and how I did have been worth a fortune to me. Those underpinnings helped me obtain and sustain riches: a beautiful, loving and faithful wife, a daughter, friends, relatives, the comforts life and the happiness they have brought.

Occasionally I have to wonder why I have been so blessed. I have no answer other than He loves us all. For my entire life, God has been coaching me to do the right things and steering me away from those things that would harm me and those I loved. At times I flirted so willingly with temptations that I could have been testing Him, but He did not relent in his love. What He did worked out well for me and those I hold dearest. Thank You, God.